THE MARKETS OF ASIA/PACIFIC: TAIWAN

The Asia Pacific Centre is the London-based
associate of the Survey Research Group. SRG
consists of market research companies in Hong
Kong, Singapore, Philippines, Malaysia, Indonesia,
Thailand and Australia.

THE MARKETS OF ASIA/PACIFIC

TAIWAN

The Asia Pacific Centre

Facts On File, Inc.

**460 Park Avenue South,
New York, N.Y. 10016**

Published in the United Kingdom in 1982 by Gower Publishing Company Limited, Croft Road, Aldershot, Hampshire, GU11 3HR, England.

Published in the United States of America in 1982 by Facts on File, Inc., 460 Park Avenue South, New York, N.Y. 10016.

Library of Congress Cataloging in Publication Data

Main entry under title:

The Markets of Asia/Pacific — Taiwan

  Includes index.
  1. Taiwan — Economic conditions — 1945.
  2. Taiwan — Commerce. I. Asia Pacific Centre
HC430.5.M33   330.951'24905   81-7798
ISBN 0-87196-589-5   AACR2

Printed in Great Britain

Contents

List of tables

'THE MARKETS OF ASIA PACIFIC' SERIES

The series of books under the title 'The Markets of Asia Pacific' is designed to provide an overview of some of the fastest growing and most dynamic markets in the world. The series will be periodically updated: for most countries, every two years.

An important feature of the series is the release for the first time of the banks of market data owned by the Survey Research Group of companies (SRG). SRG is the largest group of market research companies operating in the Asia Pacific region and heavy investment in syndicated research of their own has led to a considerable amount of new market research information now becoming available. Almost all the SRG information published in this series will not be found in any other published source.

Where SRG information exists, it has considerable depth but it covers by no means all the markets of interest. It has therefore been supplemented by key published statistics from elsewhere. The selection of published statistics has been derived from a search of existing data sources. While it is clearly beyond the scope of the series to quote from all sources found, a listing of titles and locations is included as an important feature in each country book.

In setting a style for the series, emphasis has been put on the provision of hard information rather than interpretative discussion. Wherever possible, however, key points of market development are described in the text. In effect, this is designed as a reference series which should provide mostly numeric answers to a range of marketing questions. To facilitate reference an index is provided at the back of the book.

The broad format of each country book is similar but there is some variation in specific content. This is determined by the particular market characteristics of the country and the data that happens to be available.

TAIWAN

This volume draws heavily on a large scale survey conducted by the Survey Research Group company - SRH Ltd. This is the first occasion on which most of this information has been released for general publication and it provides an overview of the main media and consumer markets as well as background demographic information. We acknowledge the data provided by SRH Ltd and their help in identifying market trends and characteristics. (Since the time of this survey the SRH Taiwan research operations have been consolidated into a new Taiwan based research company - Survey Research Asia Pacific (Taiwan) Ltd).

Most of the remaining information in this book has been derived from Taiwan Government publications. Taiwan is well provided with a wide range of up-to-date statistics from Government Departments and official bodies and our use of these statistics is gratefully acknowledged.

Individual sources used for this volume are referenced in the appropriate chapter.

In producing this book the intention has been to provide hard, statistical information across a range of markets and where possible to include information of our own.

It is proposed to up-date this volume on a two yearly basis. For the interim, the statistics selected should provide the reader with at least a good indication of the main parameters of the markets. Where the latest figures are essential, the reader is invited to refer to The Asia Pacific Centre who will either provide them or indicate the best source.

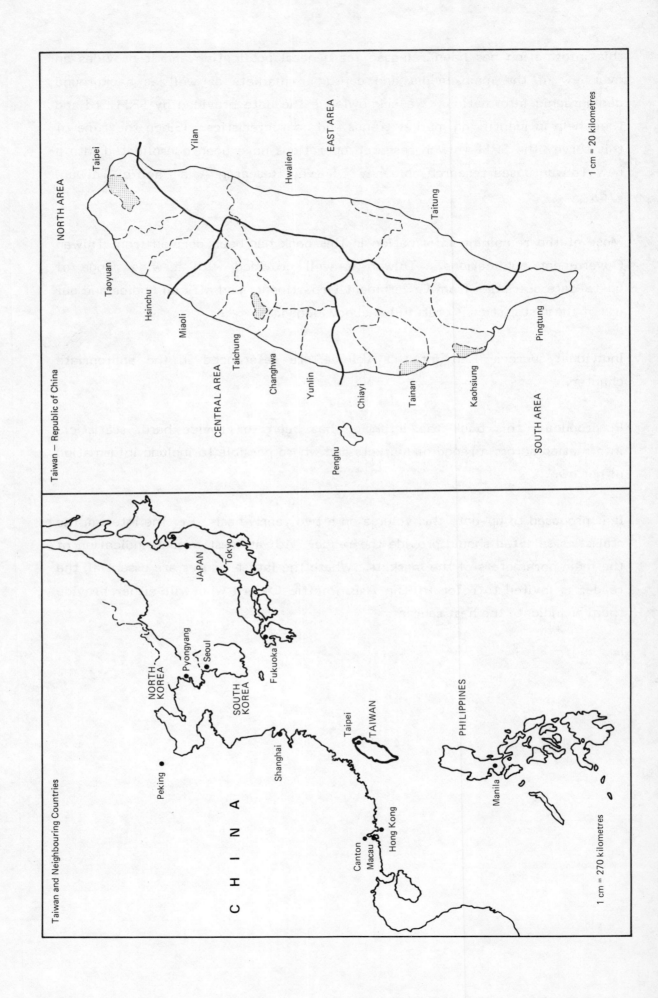

Taiwan – Republic of China

NORTH AREA

Taipei

Taoyuan

Yilan

Hsinchu

Miaoli

CENTRAL AREA

Taichung

Changhwa

Yunlin

Chiayi

Tainan

Kaohsiung

Pingtung

SOUTH AREA

Hwalien

Taitung

EAST AREA

Penghu

1 cm = 20 kilometres

Taiwan and Neighbouring Countries

C H I N A

Peking

Shanghai

Canton

Macau

Hong Kong

NORTH KOREA

Pyongyang

Seoul

SOUTH KOREA

Fukuoka

JAPAN

Tokyo

Taipei

TAIWAN

PHILIPPINES

Manila

1 cm = 270 kilometres

1 Economic and political background

THE LAND

Taiwan - familiar to many westerners by the name Formosa - is an island in the Pacific situated 100 miles from the south east coast of mainland China. The island, shaped like a tobacco leaf, is 384 kilometres long and 128 wide at its broadest point. With a total land area of 36,000 square kilometres it is a little larger in size than Massachusetts and Connecticut combined and a little smaller than the Netherlands. As well as the main island there are 13 smaller islands in the Taiwan group and a further 64 in the Penghu group. Taiwan's largest city, its commercial centre and its seat of government is Taipei which is situated in the extreme north.

The country is not well endowed with natural resources. Only 25% of the land is arable and over 60% of this has to be irrigated. Most of the remainder is rugged, mountainous terrain dominated by a spine like ridge of steep mountains running along the East coast. Minerals are scarce although there are some deposits of coal, limestone, marble and dolomite. In 1981, proven reserves of coal were 200 million tons, with 27.5 billion cubic metres of natural gas. Oil reserves are trivial - estimated in 1981 at 124.5 million bbls:- the equivalent of about two weeks of production for Saudi Arabia at its 1980 level.

64% of the land is forested and reserves at 1980 stood at 241 million cubic metres. However, forest resources are limited because of poor accessibility, inferior quality and understocking.

On a somewhat brighter note, the climate is sub-tropical which permits year round farming and usually three crops from a wide range of agricultural products, including rice, sugar cane, sweet potatoes, tea, bananas, pineapples, mushrooms and asparagus.

HISTORY

The original inhabitants of Taiwan are thought to be of Malay descent. There are still some 150,000 of these aborigines living in the rural mountainous areas. There was large scale Chinese immigration to Taiwan from the seventeenth to nineteenth centuries and in 1887 Taiwan was made a separate province of China. There followed a period of Japanese colonisation from 1895 until the end of the Second World War in 1945.

In 1949 the Chinese Nationalists - the Kuomintang under Chiang Kai-Shek - were defeated on Mainland China and retreated to Taiwan. From Taiwan's point of view the Republic of China is one entity, including the mainland, with the present Central Government in Taiwan and an opposing communist occupation of the mainland.

There has been continuing confrontation of both arms and propaganda since 1949 up until the United States' derecognition of Taiwan in 1979 as part of a rapprochement policy with the People's Republic of China on the mainland. From that time Peking has made a number of friendly overtures to Taiwan concerning reunification. These have been viewed with suspicion by the Tawainese government and to date have been emphatically rejected.

Meanwhile the Taiwan economy has - by world standards - been flourishing.

ECONOMIC DEVELOPMENT

The past 30 years has seen Taiwan move from a predominantly agricultural economy to one that is now very largely industrialised. Furthermore, its plans for the Eighties make it clear that it is aiming for the top industrial league and the fundamental question is whether there may be some overreaching given its need to import most of its energy and the timing of the next developmental burst against a world recessionary period.

Up until 1960 the emphasis was largely on agriculture with particular efforts to raise agricultural productivity and rural living standards. At the same time labour intensive, import-substituting industries were being developed to help save foreign exchange and provide employment.

The Sixties saw the encouragement of overseas investment in Taiwan in key industries and the growth of export oriented industries which took advantage of abundant low cost labour. In this way Taiwan began to move into world markets although the agricultural sector was not ignored and the export of agricultural products was actively promoted.

With the Seventies came the realisation that a growing shortage of labour required a move to capital intensive rather than labour intensive industries. However, the capital intensive industries tend to be heavy users of energy so after the oil crisis of 1973 the emphasis moved towards technology-intensive industries. The Seventies also saw a planned improvement in the country's infrastructure with large sums being spent on new ports, airports and highways.

The Seventies saw an average real growth in GNP of 10% and although this declined to 8.1% in 1979 and 6.6% in 1980, given the world recessionary situation, this was still a strong performance. At 1980 per capita GNP stood at US$2,200.

Growth in Gross Domestic Product for the latter part of the Seventies is shown below.

Table 1 – Growth of Gross Domestic Product

	Current prices		Constant 1976 prices	
	Amount (NT$m)	% growth	Amount (NT$m)	% growth
1976	701,117	20.0	701,117	13.7
1977	816,943	16.5	769,720	9.8
1978	970,269	18.8	872,854	13.4
1979	1,164,073	20.0	940,607	7.8
1980*	1,450,477	24.6	1,004,322	6.8

Source:- Directorate General of Budget, Accounting and Statistics

In 1960, agriculture accounted for 31.6% of Taiwan's GDP with industry - broadly defined - taking only 25.7%. By 1980 industry's share of GDP had risen to 52.2% while agriculture's share had fallen to 7.7%. The following more detailed figures are available for Net Domestic Product.

Table 2 - **Breakdown of Net Domestic Product**
% of NDP

	1976	1979	1980*
Agriculture	13.4	10.4	9.1
Manufacturing	32.6	34.9	34.3
Electricity, gas, water	2.1	2.4	2.6
Construction	6.7	7.3	7.6
Transport, communication	5.8	6.0	6.4
Commerce and banking	17.1	17.3	18.3
Others	22.4	21.7	21.8

Source:- Directorate General of Budget, Accounting and Statistics

Taiwan's economy relies heavily on trade with exports of goods and services amounting to 53.6% of GDP in 1980, and imports amounting to 56.4%. These levels are among the world's highest. With expansion of government services and improved living standards consumption has been growing in absolute terms. However, as a proportion of GDP, consumption expenditure has declined from 87.3% in 1960 to 66.5% in 1980. Over the same period, capital formation has grown from 20.3% to 36.3%. In 1980 domestic savings accounted for 92% of capital formation

Table 3 - **Expenditure on Gross Domestic Product by year**
(1976 constant prices)

	1978	1979	1980*
SDP components (NT$m)			
Private consumption expenditure	422,803	465,947	494,631
Government consumption expenditure	126,576	137,655	148,197
Gross fixed capital formation	229,084	261,378	301,274
Increase in stocks	21,962	46,839	39,100
Exports of goods and services	454,808	478,830	513,507
Less - imports of goods and services	382,379	450,042	492,387
Total	**872,854**	**940,607**	**1,004,322**

Source:- Directorate General of Budget, Accounting and Statistics

With its rapid economic expansion based on cheap energy, ample low cost labour and a world-wide expansion in trade, Taiwan is now facing serious problems for the coming decade. Oil prices have escalated, labour is no longer cheap in

Taiwan (manufacturing labour costs were up 25% in 1980 alone) and a world-wide recession has dimmed the prospects for continued trade growth.

Taiwan's Ten-Year Economic Development Plan has recognised these problems and defined a strategy for overcoming them. Oil is seen as a particularly severe problem area for Taiwan in that apart from rising oil prices, Taiwan is using oil less efficiently than before. Prior to the world oil crisis (1968-73), Taiwan could raise GNP by one per cent with an increase of 1.01% in energy input. By 1977 an increase of 1.44% in energy input was required to raise GNP by one per cent.

Three major approaches are planned to solve the oil problem. The promotion of energy conservation. Shifting the industrial structure towards less energy intensive industries such as electronics, machinery, transportation equipment: (technology intensive industries are planned to take 35% of manufacturing output in 1989, from 24% in 1979). Diversifying energy sources by using coal and nuclear energy in place of oil: (Taiwan Power Company is estimating that coal's contribution will reach 31% in 1989 from 12% in 1979 while nuclear power will contribute 29% from 17% in 1979).

Taiwan's present labour problem is the curious one of a highly educated and trained work force and a dearth of unskilled labour. Unemployment in 1980 stood at just 1.23% and a quarter of the 18-21 year olds were at college or university. By 1989 it is forecast that 22% of all those employed will be graduates of secondary schools and 12% college or university graduates. The problem should ease and become an advantage with Taiwan's move to more technology intensive industries.

For the period 1969 to 1978 Taiwan's exports rose at a real average annual rate of 19.2%. However, with a slow-down in world trade the plan for the Eighties sets a more modest target of 12.5% annual growth. Even this may be hard to achieve: the first half of 1981 saw Taiwan running a solid trade deficit after 5 years of surplus. Measures planned to promote trade include:- expanding exports of high value added goods where there are few trade barriers (technology intensive goods), promoting greater diversification of both products and export markets, stimulating trade with fiscal and monetary measures and raising administrative efficiency.

The Ten-Year Economic Development Plan calls for a growth in the economy of

8% for the first five years and 7.8% for the last five years. Annual price rises are expected to be in the neighbourhood of 6%. By 1984 per capita GNP at current prices is planned to reach US$3,361.

Table 4 – Major economic targets

Item	Unit	1979	1984	1989	Average Annual Growth Rate (%)		
					'80-84	'85-89	'80-89
Economic growth rate	%	8.0	8.0	7.8	8.0	7.8	7.9
Price increase rate*	%	13.5	6.0	6.0	6.0	6.0	6.0
Rate of unemployment	%	1.3	1.3	1.3	1.3	1.3	1.3
GNP	NT$ billion at 1979 prices	1,164.1	1,710.5	2,490.1	8.0	7.8	7.9
Per capita GNP	NT$ at current prices	67,140	120,990	219,845	12.5	12.7	12.6
	US$ at current prices	1,865	3,361	6,107	12.5	12.7	12.6
Exports of goods and services	US$ billion at 1979 prices	17.6	31.7	56.6	12.5	12.3	12.4
Imports of goods and services	US$ billion at 1979 prices	17.4	31.6	56.5	12.6	12.4	12.5
Trade surplus	US$ billion at 1979 prices	0.2	0.1	0.1	-	-	-
Exports of goods and services	US$ billion at current prices	17.6	42.4	101.4	-	-	-
Imports of goods and services	US$ billion at current prices	17.4	42.4	101.2	-	-	-

* Rate of wholesale price increase

Source:- Council for Economic Planning and Development

Table 5 -   Economic Indicators

	1975	1979	1980
Gross National Product (US$billion)	15.29	32.0	40.26
Gross Domestic Product - current prices (NT$m)	584,494	1,164,073	1,450,477
Gross Domestic Product - constant 1976 prices (NT$m)	616,869	940,607	1,004,322
Annual growth rate in GNP	4.2%	8.1%	6.7%
GNP per capita (US$)	888	1,722	2,101
Manufacturing share of Net Domestic Product	29.3%	34.9%	34.3%
Total trade (US$m)	11,261	30,877	39,544
Imports	5,952	14,774	19,733
Exports	5,309	16,103	19,811
Consumer prices (annual growth)	5.2	10.3	19.0
Balance of payments (NT$m) - current account	-593	+463	-870

Source:-   Directorate General of Budget, Accounting and Statistics

Council for Economic Planning and Development

Table 6 – Annual changes in real GNP/GDP growth for selected countries (1976-80)

	1976	1977	1978	1979	1980
Percentage growth in GNP/GDP					
- Total OECD	5.2	3.7	3.7	3.3	1.0
- USA	5.8	4.9	4.4	2.3	-.75
- Japan	6.0	5.4	5.9	5.9	5.0
- West Germany	5.6	2.6	3.5	4.5	1.75
- France	5.6	3.0	3.5	3.3	1.75
- United Kingdom	2.6	2.0	3.4	1.5	-2.25
- ASEAN					
- Indonesia	6.9	7.4	6.8	4.9	7.0
- Malaysia	11.6	7.7	7.5	8.5	7.6
- Philippines	6.1	6.1	6.3	5.8	4.7
- Singapore	7.2	7.8	8.6	9.3	10.0
- Thailand	9.3	7.3	11.7	6.7	5.5
- Other					
- Hong Kong	16.7	9.8	10.0	11.5	NA
- South Korea	15.5	10.3	11.6	6.3	-5.7
- **Taiwan**	**11.5**	**8.5**	**12.8**	**8.0**	**6.8**

Source:- OECD

Official Country Reports

Central Bureau of Statistics, Indonesia

Ministry of Finance, Malaysia

Singapore 1980 Budget Report

National Economic and Social Development Board, Thailand

National Economic and Development Authority, Philippines

Economic Planning Board, South Korea

Directorate General of Budget, Accounting and Statistics, Taiwan

(The table above is compiled from OECD statistics except where it has been possible to use more up-to-date statistics from national sources. In some cases OECD statistics rely on estimates of measurements, and would be amended in later publications. Differences will sometimes be found between volumes of the 'Markets of Asia Pacific' series. Where differences occur, the figures for which a national source is quoted should be considered the more accurate).

Table 7 - Annual changes in consumer prices for selected countries (1976-80)

	1976	1977	1978	1979	1980
Percentage change in prices					
- Total OECD	8.6	8.7	7.9	9.9	12.5
- USA	5.8	6.5	7.7	9.0	12.7
- Japan	9.3	8.1	3.8	3.3	8.9
- West Germany	4.5	3.9	2.6	4.3	5.2
- France	9.6	9.4	9.1	10.7	13.6
- United Kingdom	16.5	15.9	8.3	12.2	15.9
- ASEAN					
- Indonesia	19.8	11.0	8.6	24.4	15.0
- Malaysia	2.6	4.7	4.9	3.6	7.0
- Philippines	9.2	9.9	7.3	18.8	16.5
- Singapore	-1.9	3.2	4.8	4.0	9.0
- Thailand	4.2	7.2	8.0	15.0	19.7
- Other					
- Hong Kong	3.4	5.8	5.9	11.6	15.5
- South Korea	15.4	10.1	14.4	18.3	28.7
- **Taiwan**	**2.5**	**7.0**	**5.8**	**10.3**	**19.0**

Sources:- OECD
Official Country Reports
Ministry of Finance, Malaysia
Singapore 1980 Budget Report
Bangkok Bank
Hong Kong Census and Statistics Department
National Census and Statistics Department, Philippines
Economic Planning Board, South Korea
Directorate General of Budget, Accounting and Statistics, Taiwan
Central Bureau of Statistics, Singapore

(The table above is compiled from OECD statistics except where it has been possible to use more up-to-date statistics from national sources. In some cases OECD statistics rely on estimates of measurements, and would be amended in later publications. Differences will sometimes be found between volumes of the 'Markets of Asia Pacific' series. Where differences occur, the figures for which a national source is quoted should be considered more accurate).

POLITICAL BACKGROUND

The internal political situation in Taiwan is apparently stable. The Republic of China is a constitutional democracy with a President, a National Assembly and five government branches (Yuans) performing executive, legislative, judicial, examination and control functions. Effective power is held by the President - Chiang Ching-Kuo -, the Executive Yuan, the security services and the military. The Kuomintang - the Chinese Nationalists - are the ruling party. The party is dominated by Chinese coming from the mainland in 1949 although they represent a minority of Taiwan's population.

There is a limited amount of friction between the so-called 'Mainlanders' and the majority Taiwanese nationalists which flared briefly in a riot at Kaohsiung at the end of 1979. The Taiwanese nationalists see some danger in the Kuomintangs' claimed designs upon the Chinese mainland and would prefer a Singaporean style of independence for the island. However, economic growth and improving wages and living conditions are providing a panacea for any serious political unrest.

The external threat from China has apparently receded in recent years although Taiwan remains continuously on guard and 40% of the 1981/82 budget is allocated for general administration and defence. The softening of China's stance came with the US derecognition of Taiwan and several peaceful approaches on reunification with economic (and even military) independence for Taiwan have been made by those on the mainland. Although derecognition looked like a serious blow to Taiwan at the time, trade with the US has not seriously been affected and it has provided a stimulus to Taiwan to develop a broader trade base. Despite Taiwan's outward hostility to China, indirect trade between the two countries is growing.

2 The people

In the broad context of Asia Pacific, Taiwan would be considered one of the smaller countries, although its population of about 18 million (17.878 million at March 1981) still puts it ahead of Malaysia (which has about 14 million). The population has been increasing at an average rate of 1.95% per annum through the Seventies. There was a spurt in population growth rate in 1976 to 2.22% as that was the Year of the Dragon by the Chinese lunar calendar and it is believed that babies born in that year will be very successful in life. The density of population at the end of 1980 was 495 persons per square kilometre.

In common with many other countries in the region, the population of Taiwan is a relatively young one with over 50 per cent of the population aged 24 years or younger. However there is not such a marked 'bulge' in the population age profile as with Hong Kong. Taking 5 year age categories, the growth in population becomes apparent with the 25-29's (9.7% of the 1980 population) but quickly levels off for the younger age categories (each one accounting for about 10%-11% of the 1980 population).

With its population growth rate under control and a reasonable density of population, Taiwan does not face the overcrowding problems of some of its regional neighbours.

Table 8 -   Population by sex and age

	Total
	*17.878 million
	%
Male	52.2
Female	47.8
0-14 years	32.1
15-24	22.0
25-34	16.3
35-49	14.6
50+	15.0

Source:- Ministry of Interior

* March 1981

Apart from the small indigenous population of Malay descent, almost all of the people of Taiwan have come from the Mainland of China at various times over the last three to four hundred years. However, a distinction is drawn between those 'Mainlander' Nationalist Chinese who came to Taiwan as a result of the Communist victory on the mainland in 1949, and those who had migrated, or whose descendants had migrated to Taiwan before that time.

There is still some confusion today in terms of the definition of a 'Mainlander' in Taiwan where intermarried descendents of the 1949 immigrants are concerned. However, in a 1981 study by the Survey Research Group which represented almost nine tenths of the population, a sample of people were simply asked whether they considered themselves to be 'Mainlanders' or 'Taiwanese'. The resulting estimate was that 16% of the adult population are Mainlanders. They are disproportionately in the North of the country and in the urban areas and, as the table below shows, they are somewhat better-off than the Taiwanese.

Table 9 – Origin by personal income

| | | Total Adults | None | Personal income (NT$) | | | |
				-10,000	10,000-14,999	15,000-19,999	20,000+
	('000s)	10,497	4,712	1,881	1,878	957	995
		%	%	%	%	%	%
Mainlander		16	16	15	16	18	19
Taiwanese		84	84	85	84	82	81

Source:-   SRH Taiwan Survey - 1981
Note:-   Sample population 86% of total population

Another feature of the Mainlander population is that it is disproportionately male (61% of the 15+ are male). This contributes to an overall population skew in favour of males of 109:100.

With the exception of the mountainous Eastern half of the country the population has a broad geographical distribution.   There are five principal urban areas, Taipei, Keelung, Taichung, Tainan and Kaohsiung, of which the capital Taipei is the largest but still only accounts for one eighth of the total population. Between them, these main urban areas account for 28% of the Taiwan population.

Table 10 - Regional distribution of population

		Total
		*17.878 million
		%
North		
Urban -	Taipei city	12.5
	Keelung city	1.9
Rural -	Taipei Hsien	12.7
	Taoyuan Hsien	5.9
	Hsinchu Hsien	3.6
Central		
Urban -	Taichung city	3.3
Rural -	Miaoli Hsien	3.0
	Taichung Hsien	5.7
	Changhwa Hsien	6.5
	Yunlin Hsien	4.5
	Nantau Hsien	2.9
South		
Urban -	Tainan city	3.3
	Kaohsiung city	6.8
Rural -	Chiayi Hsien	4.6
	Tainan Hsien	5.4
	Kaohsiung Hsien	5.6
	Pingtung Hsien	5.0
East		
Rural -	Taitung Hsien	1.6
	Hualien Hsien	2.0
	Yilan Hsien	2.5
Penghu	Penghu Hsien	0.6

Source:- Ministry of Interior

* March 1981

At the time of going to press, one of the most comprehensive surveys of the people of Taiwan was one carried out by the Survey Research Group company SRH in the second half of 1981 (referred to above). The survey covered not only demographic information but consumer market and media information too. Since it is referred to in other chapters of this book it is used here to provide additional demographic background for the adult population of Taiwan. The survey excluded the low population East of Taiwan, Miaoli, Nantau and the island of Penghu. It represents 86% of the total population and based on a rigorous random sample, may be taken as a reasonable reflection of Taiwan's demographic profile.

In terms of occupation, the SRH survey shows that blue collar occupations are outnumbered by white collar/trader occupations and that almost one in five of those aged 15 or over are students. Almost one third of adult women are working. There are regional variations in occupation, with professional people/- managers and skilled office workers tending to be found in the North of the country and unskilled workers and tending to be found in the South (and rural areas generally).

Table 11 – Adult occupation by sex and age

	Total Adults	Male	Female	15-19	20-24	25-29	30-44	45+
('000s)	10,497	5,477	5,020	1,377	1,668	1,510	3,156	2,787
	%	%	%	%	%	%	%	%
Professional/exec/ management	2	3	*			1	2	4
Traders/proprietors	13	21	5		4	10	21	18
Office - skilled	9	8	9	*	9	16	10	7
- unskilled	6	7	6	4	12	13	3	4
Factory/shop - skilled	5	9	1		2	14	7	4
- unskilled	13	18	8	11	21	14	13	10
Fishermen/farmers	4	5	2	*		1	3	10
Housewives	25		53		9	28	41	29
Students	18	22	13	84	40	1		
Retired	4	6	*					13
Unemployed	1	1	1	1	3	1	*	1

Source:-   SRH Taiwan Survey - 1981

Note:-   Sample population 86% of total population

With just over half of adults claiming an income at all, the average level of personal income was computed at NT$14,700 per month with 11% of adults having a monthly income in excess of NT$20,000. Personal income was highest in the urban areas at an average of NT$15,600 and while the rural average was lower at NT$13,200, the difference between urban and rural earnings is not as marked as elsewhere in the Asia Pacific region. It will be seen in a subsequent chapter that rural levels of usage of consumer goods are very close to those in the urban areas.

Table 12 - Personal income by area

	Total Adults	Urban	Sub-urban	Rural	North	Central	South
('000s)	10,497	3,383	3,698	3,416	4,409	2,385	3,703
	%	%	%	%	%	%	%
Not earning	45	49	45	41	44	40	49
Earning							
-NT$1-5,000	4	2	7	5	3	8	4
-NT$5,000-9,999	13	13	13	15	14	14	13
-NT$10,000-14,999	18	14	17	23	18	21	16
-NT$15,000-19,999	9	10	9	8	12	6	8
-NT$20,000-24,999	5	6	6	2	6	4	5
-NT$25,000-29,999	2	3	1	1	1	1	3
-NT$30,000-39,999	2	2	1	2	1	5	1
-NT$40,000-49,999	1	*	*	1	*	1	1
-NT$50,000-59,999	*	1		*	*	1	
-NT$60,000-69,999	*		*				*
Over NT$70,000	*	*			*		*
Not disclosed	1	1		1	*	*	1

Source:-   SRH Taiwan Survey - 1981

Note:-   Sample population 86% of total population

Although more than a third of adult women have a personal income, only 5% were receiving NT$15,000 or more in 1981. It is also worth noting that a higher proportion of under 25's are not earning than is the case in other parts of the region. This is a function of Taiwan's well developed system of education which is covered in more detail below. The Government's own figures for 1981 show that more than a quarter of the population between the ages of 18 and 21 are attending colleges or universities. There are obvious implications here for consumer goods aimed at the younger markets.

Table 13 - Personal income by sex and age

		Total Adults	Male	Female	15-19	20-24	25-29	30-44	45+
	('000s)	10,497	5,477	5,020	1,377	1,668	1,510	3,156	2,787
		%	%	%	%	%	%	%	%
Not earning		45	26	65	84	51	30	38	37
Earning									
-NT$1-5,000		4	4	6	1	3	1	6	7
-NT$5,000-9,999		13	11	16	12	28	14	9	11
-NT$10,000-14,999		18	27	8	3	13	36	15	18
-NT$15,000-19,999		9	15	3		2	10	15	11
-NT$20,000-24,999		5	8	1		*	6	7	7
-NT$25,000-29,999		2	3				1	2	4
-NT$30,000-39,999		2	3	1			1	3	3
-NT$40,000-49,999		1	1					1	2
-NT$50,000-59,999		*	1					1	*
-NT$60,000-69,999		*	*					1	
Over NT$70,000		*	*					*	*
Not disclosed		1	1	1	*	3	1	*	*

Source:-   SRH Taiwan Survey - 1981

Note:-   Sample population 86% of total population

The educational system is both well developed and fairly complex in structure. For the academic year 1980-81 there were 5,034 educational establishments with 4,577,147 students - just over one quarter of the entire population.

Optional education is available at kindergartens for children aged 4 to 6. At present these pre-school students account for just 4% of all students, but with the number of working women increasing and growing prosperity the numbers of kindergarten children are increasing quickly. Following kindergarten, the system of six years of free and compulsory primary education was extended in 1968 to cover three years of junior high school. School attendance through this period of education is just about 100 per cent. Because there is automatic entrance to junior high from primary, the two educational categories are classified together as 'elementary education'.

Following elementary education students may qualify for a variety of further categories of education by examination. At this level are the senior high schools, a variety of vocational establishments and the junior teacher training colleges.

Higher education is available through just over one hundred institutions including 11 universities, as well as other senior colleges and research institutes.

The educational classification system is not helped by having a strong component of private as well as public schooling which does not always fit neatly into a particular category. Some private middle schools for example still combine both junior and senior high education. In the SRH Taiwan Survey respondents were asked for a personal assessment of the level of education reached using the simplified categories shown. The most important feature of the table below - which is not affected by classification - is that the level of educational attainment declines rapidly with age - particularly for those aged 30 and above. Moreover, older women are less well educated than men, reflecting a bygone era in which women were not considered as worthwile educating as men - partly because of society's general emphasis on the male's importance as the breadwinner and partly for the practical reason that the woman was likely to leave her parental home for that of her husband's family.

Table 14 - Educational level by sex and age

	Total Adults	Male	Female	15-19	20-24	25-29	30-44	45+
('000s)	10,497	5,477	5,020	1,377	1,668	1,510	3,156	2,787
	%	%	%	%	%	%	%	%
Primary or less	26	21	31	1	2	8	37	50
Secondary	26	25	26	36	20	24	26	24
High school	31	30	32	51	39	46	24	16
College/university	16	21	10	12	38	19	11	9
Post graduate	1	2	*		1	3	1	1

Source:- SRH Taiwan Survey - 1981

Note:- Sample population 86% of total population

Another demographic feature which is relevant both to the supply of labour and to a number of consumer markets, is the relatively late age of marriage. Only 13% of those in the 20-24 years age group were married, according to the SRH survey, with the late twenties the most likely age of marriage. In terms of life cycle the twenties and early thirties are periods of quite sharp change in social behaviour and this is reflected in a number of consumer markets such as cosmetics, alcoholic beverages, home appliance purchasing where age differences in market penetration are fairly large.

Table 15 - Marital status by age

	Total Adults	15-19	20-24	25-29	30-34	35-44	45+
('000s)	10,497	1,377	1,668	1,510	1,193	1,963	2,787
	%	%	%	%	%	%	%
Married	66		13	64	89	99	98
Single/separated	34	100	87	36	11	1	2

Source:-   SRH Taiwan Survey - 1981

Note:-   Sample population 86% of total population

There can be no question that the post Second World War period has seen a very strong improvement in the living conditions of the people of Taiwan. The following chapters have a number of examples of higher real earnings and increased ownership of consumer goods. The improvement is also reflected in health and nutrition. From a life expectancy of 58 years in 1952, in 1980 it was 72.2 years. In 1952 the average daily intake of calories per person was 2,078, but this had risen to 2,820 in 1980. Over the same period the intake of protein was up from 49 to 78 grams.

There is an active participation in sporting pastimes, particularly among young adults, with badminton, swimming, basketball and cycling the most popular of sports. Having noted above the relatively late marrying age in Taiwan it is of interest that the incidence of playing sports is high up to the mid-twenties. Jogging is not one of the most popular sports but is marked as one of the few where participation peaks with those aged 45 or older.

Table 16 - Sports played by sex and age

	Total Adults	Male	Female	15-19	20-24	25-29	30-34	35-44	45+
('000s)	10,497	5,477	5,020	1,377	1,668	1,510	1,193	1,963	2,787
	%	%	%	%	%	%	%	%	%
Sports played in past 4 weeks									
- Volley ball	4	7	2	15	7	4	3	1	1
- Basketball	15	25	5	46	57	11	6	3	2
- Badminton	17	16	19	44	37	15	10	4	6
- Tennis	5	7	2	5	7	5	5	3	3
- Table Tennis	8	10	6	20	15	8	4	5	1
- Football	1	2	*	3	3	2		1	*
- Golf	1	1	*		1		1		1
- Bowling	2	3	2	2	7	2	2	1	2
- Ice-skating	1	1	*	3	2	1			
- Roller skating	1	2	1	5	4	1			
- Cycling	14	14	13	35	19	9	9	7	9
- Swimming	17	21	12	28	39	24	10	6	4
- Fishing	*	1	*	*	*	1	2		*
- Hiking	7	7	6	6	4	6	9	4	10
- Mountaineering	7	10	4	6	12	7	7	6	6
- Jogging	3	4	2	2	1	3	1	4	5
- Dancing	2	*	4	1	1	1		3	2

Source:-   SRH Taiwan Survey - 1981

Note:-   Sample population 86% of total population

Mandarin is the official language of Taiwan although the Fukien dialect is very widely spoken. English can normally be used in business dealings, but is not spoken by the large majority of ordinary people. It is unlikely, for example, that directions to taxi drivers in English will be easily followed.

The main local religions are Buddhism, Taoism and Confucianism although most of the main religions are represented in Taiwan.

At the end of 1979 there were 20,000 foreign residents in Taiwan of which the main countries represented were the USA (26%), Japan (23%) and Malaysia (18%). UK led the European countries with 2% of foreign residents.

3 Private households

For some marketing purposes the household is a more relevant planning unit than the individual person. At March 1981 there were 3.78 million households in Taiwan with an average size of 4.73 people. The geographical distribution of households is similar to that of people except that individual households tend to be larger in the rural areas. As a result the urban areas contain a larger proportion of households than they do people. For example, Taipei city has 15% of households but only 12.5% of people - the average household size in Taipei city is 3.9 persons against averages of over 5.2 persons in some of the rural areas.

From a different perspective the average household has marginally over 3 adults and about 1.5 income earners.

Government statistics put the average disposable income per household in 1979 at NT$188,407 (NT$15,700 per month) which was an increase of 21% over 1978 against an increase in the price index of 9.8%. The SRH Taiwan Survey covers income at mid 1981 and suggests an average monthly household income figure of NT$24,000 for Taiwan households, which would fit in well with a Government survey figure for April 1981 - for Taipei municipality alone - of NT$28,000. As can be seen below the SRH survey would estimate somewhat higher figures for urban areas in general.

Table 17 – Household income by area

	Total Households	Urban	Sub-urban	Rural	North	Central	South
('000s)	3,348	710	332	309	643	280	428
	%	%	%	%	%	%	%
Under NT$10,000	4	5	5	2	4	3	5
NT$10,000-14,999	17	15	18	19	16	14	20
NT$15,000-19,999	23	24	20	27	25	20	22
NT$20,000-24,999	23	21	25	22	24	22	22
NT$25,000-29,999	12	10	15	12	11	14	13
NT$30,000-39,999	12	14	11	12	12	18	9
NT$40,000-49,999	4	4	4	3	4	4	4
NT$50,000-59,999	2	4	2	2	2	3	3
NT$60,000-69,999	1	1	1	1	1	1	*
NT$70,000-89,999	*	1	*	*	*		1
NT$90,000-99,999							
Over NT$100,000	1	1	*	1	1		*
Not disclosed	*	*		*	*		*

Source:- SRH Taiwan Survey - 1981

Note:- Sample population 86% of total population

As noted in the previous chapter for personal incomes it is significant that household incomes are not very much lower in the rural areas than the urban areas. Estimates from the above survey put the urban average at NT$25,200 per month against a rural average of NT$23,600.

The table below summarises Taiwan's growing wealth through the latter part of the Seventies and the extent to which it has filtered through to the people at large for private consumption and/or savings.

Table 18 – Income, expenditure and savings

	1976	1977	1978	1979	(NT$m)
GNP	696,101	811,819	967,938	1,164,473	
National income	543,737	632,795	747,451	892,726	
Personal income	478,179	565,615	662,619	803,888	
Disposable income	446,490	527,302	612,461	731,406	
- Consumption expenditure	364,061	417,736	481,733	582,072	
- Savings	82,429	109,566	130,728	149,334	

Source:- Directorate General for Budget, Accounting and Statistics

Private consumption has been growing quickly in Taiwan. Between 1952 and 1980 the level of consumption had more than tripled in real terms, and the average annual rate of growth through the Seventies was 5.9% in real terms. Prosperity has also brought changes in consumption patterns with relatively less being spent on food and more on housing, education and recreation.

Table 19 - Distribution of household consumption expenditure by year

Expenditure items	1952 %	1970 %	1980 %
- Food	55.6	42.6	35.5
- Beverages and tobacco	6.4	8.6	7.5
- Clothing and personal effects	5.5	5.3	5.4
- Housing	18.9	25.0	26.9
- Transport	1.4	2.7	5.0
- Education and entertainment	12.2	15.8	19.7

Source:-   Council for Economic Planning and Development

The Taipei City Government also runs a panel selected to represent the Taipei Municipality which reports family income and expenditure. The distribution of expenditure shown in this survey (see below) differs from the country distribution as a whole by having a higher proportionate expenditure on housing and related items. In April 1981 the Taipei survey was showing a balance between total income and total expenditure of almost NT$6,000 for the month. In the table shown below income refers to income from all sources while non-consumption expenditure includes items such as tax, interest and donations.

Table 20 - Breakdown of household expenditure in Taipei Municipality

		1976		1981
Total income	NT$	13,179	NT$	28,052
Consumption expenditure		10,896		19,492
Non-consumption expenditure		824		2,653
Balance		1,459		5,907

Per cent of consumption expenditure on

	1976	1981
- Food	40.4%	37.0%
- Beverage	0.8	1.0
- Tobacco	0.6	0.6
- Clothing and other personal effects	5.5	4.8
- Rent and water charges	23.6	24.9
- Fuel and light	4.0	5.0
- Furniture and household equipment	2.5	2.9
- Household operation	1.8	3.1
- Medical care	3.7	3.5
- Transport and communication	4.1	6.8
- Education and entertainment	7.7	6.3
- Miscellaneous	5.2	4.3

Source:-   Bureau of Budget, Accounting and Statistics, Taipei City Government

A good indication of the wealth available to private households is the level of penetration of consumer goods markets and this can be seen in subsequent chapters. However, as an indication of how things have changed over the period 1952-80:- the number of telephones per 1,000 people rose from 3.9 to 177.8, the percentage of households using electricity rose from 35.4% to 99.8% and the number of automobiles and bicycles per 1,000 people rose from 1.3 to 262.0.

At the same time there has been a levelling out in the distribution of wealth. The ratio between the income of the highest 20 per cent and that of the lowest 20 per cent stood at 15.0 to 1 in 1952 but had fallen to 5.33 to 1 in 1964 and in 1980 the figure had declined to 4.17 to 1. Educational and training opportunities, ample employment, land reform and social mobility are among the main factors accounting for this trend during a period of sustained economic growth.

Approximately 9 in every 10 homes in Taiwan are owner occupied. The figure is marginally lower in the less well-off and urban areas. In regional terms this level of ownership is very high. For example, the equivalent figure for Hong Kong is 25% and Singapore - which has emphasised home ownership in

Government planning - is 50%.

Table 21 - Ownership of home by household income

	Total Adults	-15,000	Household income (NT$) 15,000-19,999	20,000-24,999	25,000-29,999	30,000+
('000s)	10,497	2,230	2,412	2,510	1,269	2,052
	%	%	%	%	%	%
Home owned	90	82	90	92	95	93
Home rented	10	18	10	8	5	7

Source:- SRH Taiwan Survey - 1981

From the point of view of marketing consumer goods, it is relevant to look at the profile of the Taiwanese 'housewife'. The definition used in the SRH Taiwan survey for a housewife is the person mainly responsible for making the household's shopping decisions. In 14% of cases this person was found to be male - either where no female existed in the home or where the shopping was left to a male member anyway. This level of male housewife activity is similar to that of other countries in the region.

Nevertheless, the majority of housewives are female and their age profile is elderly by comparison with the population as a whole. There are two important implications of this. First, the Taiwanese housewife is likely to be more susceptible to traditional values and slower to accept new values than for example younger people buying personal goods for themselves. Second, levels of education (and English literacy) are lower among housewives which is a consideration for the planning of advertising and packaging.

Table 22 - Profile of household shopping decision maker

		Total Adults	Household shopping decision makers
		%	%
Male		52	14
Female		48	86
15-24		29	10
25-34		25	35
35-44		19	29
45+		27	27
Education	- primary or less	26	39
	- secondary/high school	57	51
	- tertiary	17	10

Source:- SRH Taiwan Survey - 1981

4 Consumer markets — non-durables

In this and the following chapter, the objective is to provide a brief summary of the main consumer markets:- that is, those in which the advertising and research expenditure tends to be high. For each market covered, size - in terms of numbers of consumers - is given together with an indication of the leading brands, where information is available. The leading brands are listed in order of their market share - again in terms of numbers of consumers.

Most of the information in these two chapters has come from the SRH Taiwan Survey (referred to earlier) of August 1981 and again attention is drawn to the fact that this survey excludes the mountainous and less populated East of the country as well as several other less populated areas. It, nevertheless, covers 86% of the total population and provides the best available estimation of market penetration for the products shown below.

The SRH Taiwan Survey is the company's first generally available survey of such size and scope and does not therefore provide indications of market trend (although this is planned for future years). The general impression from those involved in Taiwan's consumer markets is that they have either been growing in recent years or are now offering considerable potential for growth. There are serious practical problems of protecting trade marks and there have been difficulties for international companies wanting to withdraw funds from Taiwan. However, with growing affluence among the people at large, more education, more exposure to Western media, TV programmes, periodicals and very healthy investments in advertising, the potential for consumer market off-take is certainly creating considerable international interest in Taiwan as a possible development area.

There are indications of market growth already.

In the next chapter figures are quoted from the Taiwan Power Company Survey, which is repeated every two years and has shown solid growth in consumer durable ownership. The table below shows the growth rate in real terms of private consumption expenditure through the Seventies.

Table 23 - Growth rate of private consumption expenditure

	Annual growth rate (%) in real terms
1970	7.6
1971	8.1
1972	9.8
1973	11.6
1974	4.3
1975	6.9
1976	6.9
1977	6.8
1978	8.7
1979	10.2
1980*	6.2

Source:-   Directorate Generale of Budget, Accounting and Statistics

At current prices total private consumption expenditure for 1980 is estimated at NT$733,545 million: 51% of GDP which is a low proportion by international standards (eg Thailand 66% in 1978, USA 64%, Japan 58%, UK 59%).

The Asia Pacific region is made up of countries each with its own rich cultural heritage, and Taiwan is no different in having a strong Chinese character in which many forms of social behaviour have changed little over the years. The growth of international consumer brands in these markets in some ways represents a challenge to traditional values and stereotypes. It is possible to track the growing influence of Western products and more Western style values across the region and there appears to be a correlation with economic growth. One of the most interesting questions about Taiwan's consumer markets is not so much their state today but the ways in which they will change over the next decade - particularly if advertising input continues to grow. We certainly expect to see greater emphasis on user image, life style, prestige and the more psychological than physical product values, particularly in the younger market sectors.

Having said this Taiwan's traditional Chinese character will remain as the foundation for consumer market growth and any company about to involve itself in consumer marketing will need to investigate the social and cultural backgrounds which might prevail. It is beyond our scope here to provide a detailed sociological analysis of Taiwan, but some of the specific topics which could need investigation are as follows:-

- medical theory:- there are strong traditional views about what is good and bad for the body and there are a large number of topics which work in varying ways. It will also be useful to know about the concepts of 'heaty' and 'cooling'. The traditional theory is that certain food, drink or behaviour creates fire or water in the body and, depending on the body's state of balance of these elements, certain products may be appropriate or inappropriate.

- religion does not have a major impact on consumer markets in Taiwan - certainly not to the extent that Islam restricts Moslem consumption in other parts of the region.

- however there are superstitions and anxieties associated with certain colours and there is a relative preoccupation with the symbolism of brand names and their ease of pronunciation.

- certain flavours tend to be disliked.

- main meals are carefully planned for balance, flavour and food value and yet there is much snack eating where these considerations are not so important.

Those presently marketing consumer goods in Taiwan are putting more emphasis on market segmentation for brand development and in this respect age is a particularly important variable. Not only does age discriminate markets in terms of natural life cycle stages (eg starting work, marriage, starting a family) but it identifies younger markets with a broader education which are emerging with new sets of values. At the same time, the younger end of the population represents numerically larger market opportunities.

Fresh milk

Table 24 – Market summary by sex, age and household income

	Total Adults	Male	Female	15-19	20-24	25-29	30-44	45+	Household income (NT$) -19,999	20,000-29,999	30,000+
('000s)	10,497	5,477	5,020	1,377	1,668	1,510	3,156	2,787	4,642	3,779	2,052
Market penetration - consumed in past 4 weeks	36	37	34	47	52	34	31	26	30	38	45

Leading brands:- Weichuan, TPFA, Foremost, President

Source:-   SRH Taiwan Survey - 1981

Market comment:- In regional terms the market for milk products is large and milk has traditionally not been seen as a favourite with the Chinese because of its 'cheesy' after taste. However, the milk consumption habit was reinforced during 50 years of Japanese colonialisation up to the end of the Second World War. Milk is seen as a nutritious drink and consumption is particularly encouraged for young children and young adults. Weichuan is the leading brand by a long way.

Other liquid milk

Table 25 – Market summary by sex, age and household income

	Total Adults	Male	Female	15-19	20-24	25-29	30-44	45+	Household income (NT$) -19,999	20,000-29,999	30,000+
('000s)	10,497	5,477	5,020	1,377	1,668	1,510	3,156	2,787	4,642	3,779	2,052
	%	%	%	%	%	%	%	%	%	%	%
Market penetration - consumed in past 4 weeks	13	14	12	22	16	15	9	10	9	15	20

Leading brands:- Weichuan, President, Foremost

Source:-   SRH Taiwan Survey - 1981

Market comment:- As defined, this market is essentially the flavoured milk products including soya bean milk and the yoghurt drinks like Yakult. Chocolate is the most popular flavour, although soya-bean - which adds to the nutritional content - is also commonly consumed. Apple is another popular flavour. Flavoured milk is a less serious product than ordinary fresh milk and it does not have quite such a young consumer profile.,

Powdered milk

Table 26 – Market summary by sex, age and household income

| | Total Adults | Male | Female | 15-19 | 20-24 | 25-29 | 30-44 | 45+ | Household income (NT$) | | |
									-19,999	20,000-29,999	30,000+
('000s)	10,497	5,477	5,020	1,377	1,668	1,510	3,156	2,787	4,642	3,779	2,052
	%	%	%	%	%	%	%	%	%	%	%
Market penetration - consumed in past 4 weeks	56	50	62	57	55	61	60	48	49	61	61

Leading brands:- Klim, Weichuan, Red Cow
Source:-   SRH Taiwan Survey - 1981

Market comment:- Powdered milk is the most popular of the milk products. It offers greater economy but nevertheless has a strong nutritional image. Its consumer profile is less extreme in terms of age and income than fresh milk. It is used both as an additive to other drinks and as a drink in its own right. Rural market penetration (51%) is not far behind urban penetration (57%). Klim is a very solid market leader.

Instant coffee

Table 27 - Market summary by sex, age and household income

| | Total Adults | Male | Female | 15-19 | 20-24 | 25-29 | 30-44 | 45+ | Household income (NT$) | | |
									-19,999	20,000-29,999	30,000+
('000s)	10,497	5,471	5,020	1,377	1,668	1,510	3,156	2,787	4,642	3,779	2,052
	%	%	%	%	%	%	%	%	%	%	%
Market penetration - consumed in past 4 weeks	13	13	14	14	23	16	10	10	10	13	20

Leading brands:- Nescafe, Mocca

Source:-   SRH Taiwan Survey - 1981

Market comment:- For the Chinese instant coffee is seen as a stimulant and this has tended to work against any rapid growth in popularity. Parents would be somewhat wary of their children consuming coffee and it is not surprising that the market peaks with young middle-aged adults. The market is also skewed to the better-off and those in white collar occupations. While Nescafe is the clear market leader, Mocca is a very solid minority brand.

Health food drinks

Table 28 - Market summary by sex, age and household income

| | Total Adults | Male | Female | 15-19 | 20-24 | 25-29 | 30-44 | 45+ | Household income (NT$) | | |
									-19,999	20,000-29,999	30,000+
('000s)	10,497	5,471	5,020	1,377	1,668	1,510	3,156	2,787	4,642	3,779	2,052
	%	%	%	%	%	%	%	%	%	%	%
Market penetration - consumed in past 4 weeks	13	11	16	12	17	15	17	9	9	15	20

Leading brands:- Horlicks, Ovaltine

Source:-   SRH Taiwan Survey - 1981

Market comment:- In terms of consumer perception the health food drinks market is close to the milk product markets but further along a dimension of filling/nutritious. These are more expensive than milk products and have a markedly upper income profile. The market is almost completely dominated by Horlicks and Ovaltine.

Carbonated soft drinks

Table 29 - Market summary by sex, age and household income

	Total Adults	Male	Female	15-19	20-24	25-29	30-44	45+	Household income (NT$) -19,999	20,000-29,999	30,000+
('000s)	10,497	5,471	5,020	1,377	1,668	1,510	3,156	2,787	4,642	3,779	2,052
	%	%	%	%	%	%	%	%	%	%	%
Market penetration - consumed in past 4 weeks	83	85	80	83	90	85	81	78	80	86	84

Leading brands:- Hey Song, Cherice

Source:-   SRH Taiwan Survey - 1981

Market comment:- Carbonated soft drinks are extremely popular and the market is very solid with children under 15 as well as with adults. Neither of the big international colas have more than a few per cent of this market while Hei Song is a dominant brand leader. The most popular flavours are lemon and sarsparilla.

Juices

Table 30 - Market summary by sex, age and household income

	Total Adults	Male	Female	15-19	20-24	25-29	30-44	45+	Household income (NT$) -19,999	20,000-29,999	30,000+
('000s)	10,497	5,477	5,020	1,377	1,668	1,510	3,156	2,787	4,642	3,779	2,052
	%	%	%	%	%	%	%	%	%	%	%
Market penetration - consumed in past 4 weeks	33	33	33	32	42	35	35	25	26	37	41

Leading brands:- Sunkist, President, Tsin Tsin, Weichuan, Honey

Source:-   SRH Taiwan Survey - 1981

Market comment:- The market includes fruit juices in both cans and paper packs, but it is the paper pack products which have grown most in recent years. The market tends to be higher income but rural penetration is just as high as urban. Sunkist is a clear leader, but the market is fairly fragmented. Orange is by far the favourite flavour but the market also offers traditional flavours such as chrysanthemum - which is thought to have special 'cooling' properties.

Cod liver oil/capsules

Table 31 - Market summary by sex, age and household income

	Total Adults	Male	Female	15-19	20-24	25-29	30-44	45+	Household income (NT$) -19,999	20,000-29,999	30,000+
(000's)	10,497	5,477	5,020	1,377	1,668	1,510	3,156	2,787	4,642	3,779	2,052
	%	%	%	%	%	%	%	%	%	%	%
Market penetration - consumed in past 4 weeks	4	4	4	7	4	4	4	4	3	5	7

Leading brands:- Hargba, Fisherman

Source:-   SRH Taiwan Survey - 1981

Market comment:- Cod liver oil capsules are consumed by children as a source of nutrition but some adults also take them when they feel extra nutrition is needed. The peak at 15-19 shown above reflects the tail of the children's market. Among adults cod liver oil is also relatively popular with the higher income earners.

Instant noodles

Table 32 – Market summary by sex, age and household income

	Total Adults	Male	Female	15-19	20-24	25-29	30-44	45+	Household income (NT$) -19,999	20,000-29,999	30,000+
(000's)	10,497	5,477	5,020	1,377	1,668	1,510	3,156	2,787	4,642	3,779	2,052
	%	%	%	%	%	%	%	%	%	%	%
Market penetration - consumed in past 4 weeks	22	19	27	44	32	19	17	15	19	22	31

Source:-   SRH Taiwan Survey - 1981

Market comment:- Instant noodles are a relatively new product of the last decade and an example of a successful development of a convenience food where eating habits are well developed and snack foods readily available. The market is at its strongest with young adults:- the products are very popular with students.

Biscuits

Table 33 – Market summary by sex, age and household income

	Total Adults	Male	Female	15-19	20-24	25-29	30-44	45+	Household income (NT$) -19,999	20,000-29,999	30,000+
	%	%	%	%	%	%	%	%	%	%	%
Market penetration - consumed in past 4 weeks	38	31	46	54	42	34	37	33	32	43	44

Source:-   SRH Taiwan Survey - 1981

Market comment:- Biscuits like instant noodles, are more popular with women and students for whom they represent a snack food. Biscuits in tins are also a popular gift item.

Chocolate confectionery

Table 34 - Market summary by sex, age and household income

	Total Adults	Male	Female	15-19	20-24	25-29	30-44	45+	Household income (NT$) -19,999	20,000-29,999	30,000+
('000s)	10,497	5,477	5,020	1,377	1,668	1,510	3,156	2,787	4,642	3,779	2,052
	%	%	%	%	%	%	%	%	%	%	%
Market penetration - consumed in past 4 weeks	15	12	18	26	25	15	10	10	11	17	21

Source:-   SRH Taiwan Survey - 1981

Market comment:- For the Chinese, chocolate is a heaty foodstuff and consequently there is seasonability in consumption with winter peaking. This coincides with Chinese New Year purchasing of chocolates for gifts. The market is relatively strong with students and unskilled workers. However, penetration is just as high in rural as urban areas.

Sugar confectionery

Table 35 - Market summary by sex, age and household income

	Total Adults	Male	Female	15-19	20-24	25-29	30-44	45+	Household income (NT$) -19,999	20,000-29,999	30,000+
(000's)	10,497	5,477	5,020	1,377	1,668	1,510	3,156	2,787	4,642	3,779	2,052
	%	%	%	%	%	%	%	%	%	%	%
Market penetration - consumed in past 4 weeks	10	9	12	18	11	12	10	5	9	13	10

Source:-   SRH Taiwan Survey - 1981

Market comment:- Sugar confectionery is similar to chocolate in having both a gift and personal consumption sector. The age profile is young but less markedly so than for chocolate and there is less of an income skew. There is some concern among mothers that sugar confectionery can cause phlegm and aggravate coughs which inhibits the children's market somewhat. In terms of occupation the market is stronger with blue collar workers.

Analgesics

Table 36 – Market summary by sex, age and household income

	Total Adults	Male	Female	15-19	20-24	25-29	30-34	45+	Household income (NT$) -19,999	20,000-29,999	30,000+
(000's)	10,497	5,477	5,020	1,377	1,668	1,510	3,156	2,787	4,642	3,779	2,052
	%	%	%	%	%	%	%	%	%	%	%
Market penetration – consumed in past 4 weeks	11	10	12	5	6	4	13	18	11	10	13

Source:-   SRH Taiwan Survey - 1981

Market comment:- Analgesics are well established in Taiwan with a market that is elderly but not particularly well-off. The occupational groups where penetration is highest are farmers/fishermen (25% in past 4 weeks), professionals/executives (17%) and unskilled blue collar workers (16%). Rural penetration is significantly higher than urban penetration.

Vitamin pills

Table 37 – Market summary by sex, age and household income

	Total Adults	Male	Female	15-19	20-24	25-29	30-44	45+	Household income (NT$) -19,999	20,000-29,999	30,000+
(000's)	10,497		5,477	5,020	1,377	1,668	1,510	3,156	2,787	4,642	3,779
	%	%	%	%	%	%	%	%	%	%	%
Market penetration – consumed in past 4 weeks	3	3	3	3	2	3	2	3	1	3	6

Source:-   SRH Taiwan Survey - 1981

Market comment:- While penetration of the vitamin pill market is generally there are some interesting peaks. For example, past 4 week consumption reaches 7% with Mainlanders, 9% with professionals/executives and 6% for those with college/post graduate education. This is a market in which it is very relevant to understand the role of traditional products such as herbs or animal extract in physical well-being.

Beer

Table 38 – Market summary by sex, age and household income

	Total Adults	Male	Female	15-19	20-24	25-29	30-44	45+	Household income (NT$) -19,999	20,000-29,999	30,000+
(000's)	10,497	5,477	5,020	1,377	1,668	1,510	3,156	2,787	4,642	3,779	2,052
	%	%	%	%	%	%	%	%	%	%	%
Market penetration - consumed in past 4 weeks	38	57	17	21	32	43	42	43	34	40	44

Source:- SRH Taiwan Survey - 1981

Market comment:- Beer is a cooling drink and consumption is seasonal. The above figures refer to a summer period. In terms of occupation, consumption peaks with skilled (i.e. generally older) blue collar workers, and traders/proprietors. There is not much of an income bias in the market and rural penetration is as strong as urban. However, in common with a number of other consumer markets, the central region of Taiwan has a significantly lower penetration.

Chinese wine

Table 39 - Market summary by sex, age and household income

	Total Adults	Male	Female	15-19	20-24	25-29	30-44	45+	Household income (NT$) -19,999	20,000-29,999	30,000
(000's)	10,497	5,477	5,020	1,377	1,668	1,510	3,156	2,787	4,642	3,779	2,052
	%	%	%	%	%	%	%	%	%	%	%
Market penetration - consumed in past 4 weeks	16	27	4	3	8	16	17	26	15	14	21

Source:-   SRH Taiwan Survey - 1981

Market comment:- Chinese wine is a distilled spirit and the country's traditional alcoholic beverage. The misnomer 'wine' has developed because in Chinese there is one generic term for alcholic beverage which has taken the general term 'wine'. Chinese wine has remained the leading spirit in Taiwan by a long way, although in other parts of the region it has been overtaken by brandy. The market is relatively elderly and much stronger in the North (and among Mainlanders).

Other alcoholic beverages

Table 40 - Market summary by sex, age and household income

	Total Adults	Male	Female	15-19	20-24	25-29	30-44	45+	Household income (NT$) -19,999	20,000-29,999	30,000+
(000's)	10,497	5,477	5,020	1,377	1,668	1,510	3,156	2,787	4,642	3,779	2,052
	%	%	%	%	%	%	%	%	%	%	%
Market penetration - consumed in past 4 weeks											
Other brandy	1	1	1	2	*	*	1	2	*	1	2
Gin	*	*	*	1				*	*	*	
Scotch whisky	1	1	1	2	*		1	1	*	1	1
Other whisky	1	1	1	*	1	1	*	2	*	1	2

Source:-   SRH Taiwan Survey - 1981

Market comment:- No other spirits have made any impact to date on the Taiwan market, although there are precedents elsewhere in the region for much more substantial market penetration among Chinese consumers. Brandy has the traditional image of being a heaty, strengthening spirit while whisky has a less positive image of being cooling and if anything weakening the body.

Cigarettes

Table 41 - Market summary by sex, age and household income

	Total Adults	Male	Female	15-19	20-24	25-29	30-44	45+	Household income (NT$) -19,999	20,000-29,999	30,000+
(000's)	10,497	5,477	5,020	1,377	1,668	1,510	3,156	2,787	4,642	3,779	2,052
	%	%	%	%	%	%	%	%	%	%	%
Market penetration - consumed in past 4 weeks	37	65	6	10	33	39	38	51	37	36	39

Source:- SRH Taiwan Survey - 1981

Market comment:- A high penetration market in regional terms (cf about a quarter of adults smoking in Hong Kong) with no income bias but an elderly smoker profile. The incidence of smoking in the past 4 weeks is highest with the skilled artisans (77%), the professionals/executives (72%) and the traders (68%). There is no regional or urban/rural skew to the market.

Toiletries

Table 42 - Market summary by sex, age and household income

	Total Adults	Male	Female	15-19	20-24	25-29	30-44	45+	Household income (NT$) -19,999	20,000-29,999	30,000+
(000's)	10,497	5,477	5,020	1,377	1,668	1,510	3,156	2,787	4,642	3,779	2,052
	%	%	%	%	%	%	%	%	%	%	%
Market penetration - consumed in past 4 weeks											
Shampoo	95	91	100	96	99	100	96	88	94	96	94
Talcum powder	17	13	21	28	19	18	17	10	13	18	23
Bath additives	2	1	3	3	2	3	1	1	*	2	4
Hair conditioner	27	11	44	26	39	37	28	14	23	31	30

Source:-   SRH Taiwan Survey - 1981

Market comment:- The shampoo market has almost reached saturation and the hair conditioner market has been growing steadily in recent years. Both markets reflect an increasing concern with the appearance and feel of hair rather than simply cleaning it. Specialist bath additives compete with disinfectant. Talcum powder has a higher penetration in rural than urban areas. The reverse is true of hair conditioner. Hair conditioner penetration is 43% with unskilled office workers.

After-shave/cologne

Table 43 - Market summary by age and household income

	Total Men	15-19	20-24	25-29	30-44	45+	Household income (NT$) -19,999	20,000-29,999	30,000+
(000's)	5,477	738	848	750	1,373	1,767	2,438	1,942	1,075
	%	%	%	%	%	%	%	%	%
Market penetration - used in past 4 weeks	15	4	2	15	21	20	11	15	23

Source:-   SRH Taiwan Survey - 1981

Market comment:- Penetration peaks in the professional/executive occupation at 51% (used in past 4 weeks). Personal income is another important market variable:- 43% of those earning NT$20,000 or more a month used after-shave/-cologne in the past 4 weeks against only 12% of those earning NT$15,000-19,999. Penetration is more than twice as high among married than single men.

Cosmetics

Table 44 - Market summary by age and household income

	Total Women	15-19	20-24	25-29	30-44	45+	Household income (NT$) -19,999	20,000-29,999	30,000+
(000's)	5,020	638	820	759	1,782	1,020	2,204	1,837	976
	%	%	%	%	%	%	%	%	%
Market penetration -									
used in past 4 weeks									
Face/moisturising cream	40	26	40	57	43	28	32	46	46
Hand/body lotion	10	4	14	12	8	13	5	13	16
Cleansing cream/lotion	50	39	65	70	49	32	41	57	56
Skin treatments	7	3	4	8	9	7	5	8	10
Astringent/tonic	14	2	14	30	16	9	10	18	17
Foundations	22	2	16	36	25	21	13	26	32
Face powder	23	2	19	39	27	19	17	27	27
Lipstick	37	10	33	52	46	29	27	42	48
Blush/rouge	20	1	14	28	27	19	11	27	26
Eye shadow	12	3	12	22	12	11	6	16	20
Eye liner	13	2	11	21	15	11	6	18	18
Nailpolish/ varnish	24	10	26	21	31	20	16	29	31
Perfume/cologne	19	7	26	22	18	16	10	25	27

Source:-   SRH Taiwan Survey - 1981

Market comment:- The Taiwan cosmetic markets are similar in profile to those of other parts of the region. Market penetration tends to be low in the teens - where a high proportion of girls are still studying - and builds up to a peak around the years of marriage. In the post marital years penetration falls away quite sharply in a number of markets. A question of particular interest is whether there is essentially a life cycle factor at work or whether there is a younger cohort of women - a new generation - who will maintain their use of cosmetics through middle age. Rural market penetration is only marginally lower than urban.

Hairdressing

Table 45 - Market summary by sex, age and household income

	Total Adults	Male	Female	15-19	20-24	25-29	30-44	45+	Household income (NT$) -19,999	20,000-29,999	30,000+
(000's)	10,497	5,477	5,020	1,377	1,668	1,510	3,156	2,787	4,642	3,779	2,052
	%	%	%	%	%	%	%	%	%	%	%
Market penetration - used in past 4 weeks	8	14	1	2	6	10	7	12	4	9	13

Leading brands:- VIP, Tancho

Source:- SRH Taiwan Survey - 1981

Market comment:- This is essentially a male market and one that has been declining in other parts of Asia. Although no trend data is available here, the elderly market profile suggests a decline in interest among the younger adults. The market penetration increases significantly with rising personal income (to 29% of those earning NT$20,000 or more using in the past 4 weeks). However, there are no regional or urban/rural differences in penetration.

Infant milk

Table 46 - Market summary by household income and urban/rural

	Total Households	-15,000	Household income (NT$) 15,000-19,999	20,000-24,999	25,000-29,999	30,000+	Urban	Suburban	Rural
(000's)	3,348	714	778	765	411	673	1,183	1,151	1,014
	%	%	%	%	%	%	%	%	%
Market penetration - have in home	17	16	17	19	14	19	17	17	18

Source:-   SRH Taiwan Survey - 1981

Market comment:- Lower market penetration in the central part of the country at 13%.

Áerosol insecticide

Table 47 - Market summary by household income and urban/rural

| | Total Households | Household income (NT$) | | | | | | | |
		-15,000	15,000-19,999	20,000-24,999	25,000-29,999	30,000+	Urban	Suburban	Rural
(000's)	3,348	714	778	765	411	673	1,183	1,151	1,014
	%	%	%	%	%	%	%	%	%
Market penetration - have in home	52	52	47	56	48	56	54	55	47

Source:-   SRH Taiwan Survey - 1981

Market comment:-   There is still some competition from liquid sprays and mosquito coils but aerosol insecticide is the dominant sector.   Market penetration peaks in the North at 66%.

Liquid detergent

Table 48 - Market summary by household income and urban/rural

| | Total Households | Household income (NT$) | | | | | | | |
		-15,000	15,000-19,999	20,000-24,999	25,000-29,999	30,000+	Urban	Suburban	Rural
(000's)	3,348	714	778	765	411	673	1,183	1,151	1,014
	%	%	%	%	%	%	%	%	%
Market penetration - have in home	56	38	55	62	66	63	54	61	53

Household penetration is markedly lower in the South of the country (at 39%) than in the North (69%).

Toothpaste

Table 49 – Market summary by household income and urban/rural

		Total Household	-15,000	Household income (NT$) 15,000- 19,999	20,000- 24,999	25,000- 29,999	30,000+	Urban	Suburban	Rural
	(000's)	3,348	714	778	765	411	673	1,183	1,151	1,014
		%	%	%	%	%	%	%	%	%
Market penetration - have in home		100	99	100	100	100	100	100	100	100

Leading brands:- Darkie, Kolynos, Orchid

Source:-   SRH Taiwan Survey - 1981

Market comment:- The market has reached saturation.. Darkie is an extremely dominant market leader. It is an interesting brand featuring a negroon a black, green and white outer pack. It has a strong flavour which is apparently very acceptable. Kolynos and Orchid are relatively stronger up-market.

Shampoo

Table 50 – Market summary by household income and urban/rural

		Total Household	-15,000	Household income (NT$) 15,000- 19,999	20,000- 24,999	25,000- 29,999	30,000+	Urban	Suburban	Rural
	(000's)	1,348	714	778	765	411	673	1,183	1,151	1,014
		%	%	%	%	%	%	%	%	%
Market penetration - have in home		98	95	98	99	99	99	97	99	98

Leading brands:- Nice, VO5, Kao, Clairol, Top

Source:-   SRH Taiwan Survey - 1981

Market comment:- The market is essentially a liquid shampoo one, although there is still a sizeable minority powder sector, which is popular in the lower income homes. The market is a fairly fragmented one. No single brand has more than a third of the market although Nice still has a clear lead.

Hair conditioner

Table 51 – Market summary by household income and urban/rural

	Total Household	-15,000	Household income (NT$) 15,000- 19,999	20,000- 24,999	25,000- 29,999	30,000+	Urban	Suburban	Rural
(000's)	1,348	714	778	765	411	673	1,183	1,151	1,014
	%	%	%	%	%	%	%	%	%
Market penetration - have in home	35	24	27	42	41	43	43	35	25

Source:-   SRH Taiwan Survey - 1981

Market comment:- This market is disproportionately upper income, urban and Northern. Kao - the Japanese brand - is a very dominant brand leader with a middle income profile.

Disinfectant

Table 52 – Market summary by household income and urban/rural

	Total Households	-15,000	Household income (NT$) 15,000- 19,999	20,000- 24,999	25,000- 29,999	30,000+	Urban	Suburban	Rural
(000's)	1,348	714	778	765	411	673	1,183	1,151	1,014
	%	%	%	%	%	%	%	%	%
Market penetration - have in home	10	8	9	11	7	14	14	9	7

Source:-   SRH Taiwan Survey - 1981

Market comment:- Widely used for washing and cleansing purposes. First aid use a minority. The market is disproportionately in urban areas and the North.

Toilet soap

Table 53 – Market summary by household income and urban/rural

	Total Households	-15,000	Household income (NT$) 15,000- 19,999	20,000- 24,999	25,000- 29,999	30,000+	Urban	Suburban	Rural
(000's)	1,348	714	778	765	411	673	1,183	1,151	1,014
	%	%	%	%	%	%	%	%	%
Market penetration – have in home	89	85	91	92	92	87	86	90	92

Source:-   SRH Taiwan Survey - 1981

Market comment:- Somewhat lower penetration in the South than elsewhere, but essentially a well penetrated market all round.

Powder detergent

Table 54 – Market summary by household income and urban/rural

	Total Households	-15,000	Household income (NT$) 15,000- 19,999	20,000- 24,999	25,000- 29,999	30,000+	Urban	Suburban	Rural
(000's)	1,348	714	778	765	411	673	1,183	1,151	1,014
	%	%	%	%	%	%	%	%	%
Market penetration – have in home	86	84	89	87	91	83	84	87	89

Source:-   SRH Taiwan Survey - 1981

Market comment:- 76% of houses have a washing machine. Detergent market penetration is a little lower in the South at 80% of homes.

Colour films

Table 55 – Market summary by sex, age and household income

| | Total Adults | Male | Female | 15-19 | 20-24 | 25-29 | 30-44 | 45+ | Household income (NT$) | | |
									-19,000	20,000-29,999	30,000+
('000s)	10,497	5,477	5,020	1,377	1,668	1,510	3,156	2,787	4,642	3,779	2,052
	%	%	%	%	%	%	%	%	%	%	%
Market penetration - bought in past 4 weeks	29	31	26	33	41	33	25	21	18	35	41

Leading brands:- Kodak, Fuji, Sakura

Source:- SRH Taiwan Survey - 1981

Market comment:- This is a particularly strong market among those with higher levels of education. 51% of those who reached tertiary education level had bought films in the past 4 weeks. It is also disproportionately a Mainlander market. Income is also a particularly important market factor. Kodak is the clear market leader but both Fuji and Sakura are very solid minority brands.

5 Consumer markets — durables

This chapter provides summary information for the major durable markets. Consumer durable markets have been growing quickly through the Seventies as disposable income within the household has been increasing. To take an example, in 1979 average disposable income per household was up by 21% over 1978 against an increase in prices of just 9.8% and the increase over the previous six years in disposable income was over 100 per cent.

Many of the durable markets are now approaching first stage saturation - colour televisions, refrigerators, washing machines - and future development now looks likely at a secondary stage of market refinement. For example, purchasing a second television for the home, replacing a semi-automatic with a fully automatic washing machine, replacing a refrigertor with one which has a separate freezer section.

At the time of writing some markets still have relatively low penetration and apparent growth potential; such as air conditioners, kitchen appliances, cameras, sewing machines and video recorders. Dishwashers and deep freezers have made virtually no impact so far - believed to be function of a much lower level of consumer need for these products than in the West (shops for example are very accessible with long opening hours). Also electric ovens and microwave ovens have hardly any market penetration because they do not suit the Chinese style of preparing food.

Most of the consumer durable markets are dominated by Japanese goods which have established a reputation as being both technically advanced and reliable as well as offering very competitive prices. In a number of markets Taiwan made durables are very successful but it is relatively rare to find United States or European durables in leading market positions.

Most of the figures in this chapter are taken from the SRH Taiwan Survey in the second half of 1981 (op cit). However, attention should also be drawn to a bi-annual survey conducted by the Taiwan Power Company into household ownership of various electrical appliances. The following figures are taken from the 1979 survey and allow some comparison with the 1981 SRH Taiwan Survey figures.

Table 56 – Penetration of electric household appliances

	Total Households %
Own:-	
- Electric fan	93.7
- TV set	92.0
- Electric cooker	88.9
- Refrigerator	84.8
- Washing machine	52.5
- Juice extractor	34.3
- Toaster	17.2
- Electric heater	6.1
- Air conditioner	12.1

Source:- Taiwan Power Company - 1979 Survey

Colour television

Table 57 – Market summary by household income and urban/rural

| | Total Households | Household income (NT$) | | | | | | | |
		-15,000	15,000-19,999	20,000-24,999	25,000-29,999	30,000+	Urban	Suburban	Rural
(000's)	3,348	714	778	765	411	673	1,183	1,151	1,014
	%	%	%	%	%	%	%	%	%
Market penetration - have in home	91	78	91	95	95	96	91	91	90

Leading brands:- Sony, Tatung, Sharp, National, Sanyo
Source:-   SRH Taiwan Survey - 1981

Market comment:- The market is now close to saturation. Japanese brands dominate but the Taiwanese brand - Tatung - has a very healthy market share and is particularly strong in the lower income homes. There is no single dominant brand. Sony has a marginal lead and is stronger up-market. Television has only been going for 20 years in Taiwan.

Black and white television

Table 58 - Market summary by household income and urban/rural

	Total Households	-15,000	Household income (NT$) 15,000- 19,999	20,000- 24,999	25,000- 29,999	30,000+	Urban	Suburban	Rural
(000's)	3,348	714	778	765	411	673	1,183	1,151	1,014
	%	%	%	%	%	%	%	%	%
Market penetration - have in home	12	22	9	10	8	8	11	10	13

Leading brands:- Tatung, Sanyo, Sharp, Kolin

Source:-   SRH Taiwan Survey - 1981

Market comment:- Essentially a low income market with a local brand dominating.

Radio

Table 59 - Market summary by household income and urban/rural

	Total Households	-15,000	Household income (NT$) 15,000- 19,999	20,000- 24,999	25,000- 29,999	30,000+	Urban	Suburban	Rural
(000's)	3,348	714	778	765	411	673	1,183	1,151	1,014
	%	%	%	%	%	%	%	%	%
Market penetration - have in home	59	56	55	64	56	62	64	60	52

Source:-   SRH Taiwan Survey - 1981

52

Market comment:- Perhaps a feature of the high television penetration is the somewhat low market penetration for radios:- eg over 90% of homes in Hong Kong and over 80% in Singapore have a radio. Radio listening is disproportionately by the 15-29 year olds.

Air conditioner

Table 60 - Market summary by household income and urban/rural

	Total Households	-15,000	15,000-19,999	20,000-24,999	25,000-29,999	30,000+	Urban	Suburban	Rural
(000's)	3,348	714	778	765	411	673	1,183	1,151	1,014
	%	%	%	%	%	%	%	%	%
Market penetration - have in home	22	9	18	21	25	38	33	19	11

Leading brands:- GE, National, Hitachi, Sanyo, Tatung
Source:- SRH Taiwan Survey - 1981

Market comment:- An upper income market with apparent scope for growth among middle and lower income homes and in suburban areas.

Refrigerator

Table 61 - Market summary by household income and urban/rural

	Total Households	-15,000	15,000-19,999	20,000-24,999	25,000-29,999	30,000+	Urban	Suburban	Rural
(000's)	3,348	714	778	765	411	673	1,183	1,151	1,014
	%	%	%	%	%	%	%	%	%
Market penetration - have in home	99	97	99	99	100	99	98	100	99

Leading brands:- Tatung, Sanyo, National, Sharp
Source:- SRH Taiwan Survey - 1981

Market comment:- A saturated market in which Tatung is the clear leader from a clutch of Japanese brands. Again Tatung's strength lies with the lower income homes. The market has an abundance of brands available.

Washing machine

Table 62 - Market summary by household income and urban/rural

| | Total Households | Household income (NT$) | | | | | Urban | Suburban | Rural |
		-15,000	15,000-19,999	20,000-24,999	25,000-29,999	30,000+			
(000's)	3,348	714	778	765	411	673	1,183	1,151	1,014
	%	%	%	%	%	%	%	%	%
Market penetration - have in home	76	62	75	80	79	88	83	79	66

Leading brands:- Sanyo, Tatung, National
Source:-   SRH Taiwan Survey - 1981

Market comment:- Household penetration is estimated to have gained over twenty percentage points in the last two years. The future is expected to see growth of the fully automatic machines. Sanyo has a clear lead in the market but is stronger in the North and Central areas than the South. Tatung has a solid market share - disproportionately low income.

Motor car

Table 63 – Market summary by household income and urban/rural

	Total Households	-15,000	Household income (NT$) 15,000- 19,999	20,000- 24,999	25,000- 29,999	30,000+	Urban	Suburban	Rural
(000's)	3,348	714	778	765	411	673	1,183	1,151	1,014
	%	%	%	%	%	%	%	%	%
Market penetration - have in home	11	4	5	13	14	24	16	11	7

Leading makes:- Yue Loong, Ford, Honda

Source:-   SRH Taiwan Survey - 1981

Market comment:- Government figures for 1980 show car registrations at 358,277 for private use and 67,166 for business use. These figures tie in well with the above estimate which covers 89% of all households in 1981. The market is dominated by the local make - not particularly low income in profile - and Ford, although Honda now has a solid share as a minor brand (in particular its Civic model).

Motor cycle

Table 64 – Market summary by household income and urban/rural

	Total Households	-15,000	Household income (NT$) 15,000- 19,999	20,000- 24,999	25,000- 29,999	30,000+	Urban	Suburban	Rural
(000's)	3,348	714	778	765	411	673	1,183	1,151	1,014
	%	%	%	%	%	%	%	%	%
Market penetration - have in home	65	57	61	69	75	70	54	72	71

Market comment:- Motor cycles are very popular in Taiwan, particularly in the suburban and rural areas and away from the Northern area. The Government registration figure for 1980 was 3.97 million motor cycles: implying fairly common household ownership of more than one motor cycle.

Camera

Table 65 - Market summary by household income and urban/rural

	Total Households	-15,000	Household income (NT$) 15,000- 19,999	20,000- 24,999	25,000- 29,999	30,000+	Urban	Suburban	Rural
(000's)	3,348	714	778	765	411	673	1,183	1,151	1,014
	%	%	%	%	%	%	%	%	%
Market penetration - have in home	38	19	28	43	51	58	46	40	27

Leading brands:- Canon, Nikon

Source:-   SRH Taiwan Survey - 1981

Market comment:- Cameras have such a high income market profile that with ever widening affluence in Taiwan it does look as though there is good potential for growth lower down the market. The market is considerably stronger in the North of the country. Canon is a dominant brand leader.

Piano

Table 66 – Market summary by household income and urban/rural

| | | Total Households | Household income (NT$) | | | | | | |
			-15,000	15,000-19,999	20,000-24,999	25,000-29,999	30,000+	Urban	Suburban	Rural
	(000's)	3,348	714	778	765	411	673	1,183	1,151	1,014
		%	%	%	%	%	%	%	%	%
Market penetration - have in home		3	*	3	2	2	7	4	2	2

Source:-   SRH Taiwan Survey - 1981

Market comment:- There is a growing awareness of and interest in Western style arts throughout Asia Pacific and although the penetration of pianos is low at present figures have been included as a baseline for an expected market growth. Taiwan is faced with less of a housing space problem than its neighbour Hong Kong.

Other durable appliances

Table 67 – Market summary by household income and urban/rural

| | | Total Households | Household income (NT$) | | | | | | |
			-15,000	15,000-19,999	20,000-24,999	25,000-29,999	30,000+	Urban	Suburban	Rural
	(000's)	3,348	714	778	765	411	673	1,183	1,151	1,014
		%	%	%	%	%	%	%	%	%
Market penetration - have in home										
Telephone		61	50	57	64	58	76	70	69	42
Stereo Hi-fi		24	8	21	27	31	37	29	21	21
Electric sewing machine		8	3	6	10	9	12	9	7	8
Video tape recorder		5	1	2	3	8	14	7	5	3
Mircowave oven		1	*	1	2	*	3	1	2	*

Source:-   SRH Taiwan Survey - 1981

Market comment:- The penetration of electric sewing machines is low compared with other parts of the region. Clothing is a relatively inexpensive item and tailoring/repair shops are accessible and not very expensive. Video recorders look like a market of potential with domestic production seen as unlikely in the short term (China External Trade Development Council).

Table 68 – Motor vehicle registrations

		1980 Total ('000s)
Total		**4,664.6**
Bus	- business	13.5
	- private	4.5
Motor cars	- business	67.2
	- private	358.3
Trucks	- business	33.1
	- private	203.6
Tricycle motor cars		0.5
Special purpose		10.1
Motor cycles		3,965.5
Motor 3 wheelers		8.3

Source:-   Ministry of Communications

6 Tourist markets

MARKET CHARACTERISTICS

It was sixteenth century Portuguese mariners who named Taiwan 'Ilha Formosa' - beautiful island - and today the country's scenic beauty remains the cornerstone of its attraction to visitors. Mountains, lakes, spas, gorges, botanical parks are all part of Taiwan's beauty which combine with an essentially Chinese culture which allows many glimpses of what ancient China was like.

Taiwan has benefitted through the Sixties and Seventies by a growth in regional tourism (particularly visitors from Japan) and by Mainland China's closed door policy which lasted until 1979. If the Asian tourist market is defined in terms of visitor expenditure then in 1980 Taiwan is second only to Hong Kong. The average annual growth in the number of visitors in the Sixties was 35.3% and in the Seventies 14.3%.

However, the end of the Seventies has seen a number of problems for Taiwan's tourist industry. With Japan hit by a world recession Asian tourism suffered generally, but Taiwan with its disproportionate share of Japanese visitors was hit more than most. Also, China's open door policy following the establishment of diplomatic relations with the USA is thought likely to have affected travel to Taiwan. There are no figures available to confirm this, but it so happens that Mainland China's main tourist sources are the same as Taiwans - the USA and Japan.

Taiwan's diplomatic isolation has also presented problems for tourism by creating difficulties in obtaining visas. Taiwan has no diplomatic relations with Europe which in 1979 only accounted for 3.9% of Taiwan's visitors. Another side-effect of the diplomatic situation has been difficulties faced by the national airline - China Airlines in obtaining landing rights. At present the airline has no suitable Western European route although several possibilities are under consideration, including Paris, Frankfurt and Amsterdam. (At present China Airlines does have flying rights to Luxembourg).

After a healthy rise in the number of visitors in 1978 of 14.5% over 1977, the rate of growth declined sharply in 1979 to 5.5%, and in 1980 to 3.9%.

Table 69 – Number of visitors by year

	1978	1979	1980
Total visitors (000)	1,271	1,340	1,393
Overseas Chinese (000)	225	244	282
Foreign visitors (000)	1,046	1,097	1,111
Foreign as a per cent of all visitors	82.3	81.8	79.8
Visitors index (1976=100)	126.1	133.0	138.2
Growth rate (%)	14.5	5.5	3.9

Source:-   Ministry of Communications

For the overseas Chinese in 1980, Hong Kong was by far the main source of visitors with 73.7% of all Chinese visitors. No other country accounted for more than 5%. Looking at other foreign visitors Japan remained the main source in 1980 with 58.9% despite a decline in number of 39,258. The USA accounted for 11.0% and although United States visitors increased in 1980 the number was still not back to the 1975 level and 18.5% below the 1978 level. 1980 generally saw an improvement in numbers of visitors and the only other main country also still well below its Seventies peak was Australia.

Table 70 - Foreign visitor arrivals by nationality and year

	1975	1976	1977	1978	1979	1980
Total	715,630	853,875	933,936	1,045,916	1,096,735	1,111,130
Japan	419,259	516,449	561,155	624,868	693,671	654,413
Korea, Rep. of	6,910	7,227	9,686	11,610	13,790	15,333
Malaysia	26,301	31,129	36,738	42,170	52,136	64,781
Ryukyus	-	-	-	-	-	-
Philippines	6,768	6,660	9,437	16,539	18,154	20,227
Thailand	12,625	13,681	17,040	19,911	18,888	21,729
Viet-Nam	850	89	63	506	495	41
Canada	6,782	9,016	10,672	11,972	11,822	14,396
United States	123,550	137,488	141,837	150,432	113,596	122,673
Mexico	408	492	217	350	365	388
Belgium	779	966	1,228	1,380	1,509	1,557
France	3,237	4,250	4,593	5,729	6,685	7,405
Germany, Rep. of	11,478	13,546	14,189	15,943	15,858	17,576
Italy	1,874	2,951	2,574	3,456	3,889	4,380
Netherlands	2,734	3,278	3,564	4,366	4,681	4,974
Spain	917	1,220	846	899	1,250	1,368
Switzerland	2,428	2,721	3,973	3,446	3,705	4,039
United Kingdom	14,563	15,328	16,419	19,106	20,639	21,295
Australia	12,908	16,580	16,804	16,944	12,625	12,984
New Zealand	1,343	1,296	1,381	1,748	1,654	1,851
S Africa	1,809	1,499	2,305	2,960	2,658	4,979
Others	58,107	68,009	80,104	91,581	98,665	114,741

Source:-   Ministry of Communications

It is of interest that while American foreign visitors to Taiwan declined after derecognition the numbers of overseas Chinese visitors coming from the USA hardly changed in 1979 and increased strongly in 1980.

Table 71 – Overseas Chinese arrivals by place of residence and year

	1975	1976	1977	1978	1979	1980
Total	137,510	154,251	176,246	225,061	243,647	282,124
Hong Kong	105,850	132,062	147,873	165,085	176,385	208,012
Japan	1,866	1,460	1,408	6,798	11,200	12,426
Korea, Rep. of	3,290	3,589	3,315	11,735	14,477	15,000
Malaysia	1,334	1,597	1,494	2,851	4,590	6,747
Ryukyus	-	-	-	-	-	-
Philippines	811	795	856	3,884	4,935	5,835
Singapore	1,439	954	850	3,994	5,237	5,375
Thailand	733	720	874	2,527	2,929	3,851
Viet-Nam	11,390	4,462	10,670	4,401	2,151	126
Indonesia	1,915	2,098	2,432	5,485	5,758	6,749
Brazil	194	95	76	277	463	371
Canada	334	375	413	863	668	579
United States	2,327	2,250	2,317	12,789	12,700	14,454
S Africa	3	6	6	39	26	16
Belgium	36	6	11	22	9	42
France	39	66	91	366	154	98
Germany, Rep. of	250	170	221	222	91	211
Netherlands	22	49	7	27	27	25
United Kingdom	18	23	216	158	42	88
Australia	23	87	122	246	92	176
Tahiti	119	121	120	108	7	23
Others	5,517	3,266	2,874	3,192	1,706	1,920

Source:-   Ministry of Communications

October and November are the peak months for visitor arrivals - the period of the Double Ten celebration. October in particular is a peak month for overseas Chinese to visit Taiwan. In 1979 one sixth of overseas Chinese visitors travelled to Taiwan in October.

In 1979 the average length of stay was 7.2 days, which is more than achieved by Hong Kong, Singapore, Malaysia and Thailand, but less than the Philippines. The average spending per day was US$95.22 and the total revenue from tourism for the whole of 1979 was US$919m. The average expenditure per visitor rose by 43.3% in 1979.

Table 72 – Visitor expenditure and length of stay

Year	Number of Visitors (Person)	Average Length of Stay (Day)	Spending Per Person Per Day (US$)	Spending Per Person (US$)	Total Revenue From Tourism (US$)
1968	301,770	5.59	31.58	176.53	53,271.000
1969	371,473	4.56	33.10	150.90	56,055,000
1970	472,452	4.86	35.59	172.97	81,720,000
1971	539,755	4.61	44.21	203.84	110,000,000
1972	580,033	4.58	48.44	221.89	128,707,000
1973	824,393	4.59	64.98	298.25	245,882,000
1974	819,821	4.42	76.82	339.59	278,400,000
1975	853,140	6.30	66.86	421.21	359,358,000
1976	1,008,126	6.71	68.90	462.32	466,077,000
1977	1,110,182	6.56	75.57	495.74	550,362,000
1978	1,270,977	6.75	70.87	478.37	608,000,000
1979	1,340,382	7.20	95.22	685.58	918,944,000
1980	1,393,254				

Source:-   Tourism Bureau

At the end of 1979 Taiwan had 34 international standard tourist hotels with 9,160 rooms and 91 tourist standard hotels with 8,827 rooms. The average room occupancy rate for the year was 60.3%. (The Government is changing the grading system for hotels from the above two categories to a 5 star system).

Table 73 – Hotel numbers

	1979
All hotels and lodging places	3,239
Restaurants	6,492
Eating houses	6,139
Beverage shops	3,974
Other drinking and eating places	324

Source:- Ministry of Economic Affairs

DEVELOPMENT OF TOURISM

According to Taiwan's Ten-Year Economic Development Plan the target for 1989 is 2.78 million incoming visitors: 107% up on the 1979 figure. The aggregate target for the Eighties is 21 million visitors.

The basic policies include protection for the natural landscape, building more tourist hotels, intensifying international promotion of Taiwan and also boosting domestic tourism. The Ten-Year Plan specifies six projects for tourism in the Eighties which together will involve an investment of NT$48.5 billion. The projects are as follows:-

Table 74 - Planned tourism development projects

Project	Investment in period 1980-1989 (NT$ billion)
1. Development of scenic areas	8.1
2. Development of 10 national parks	21.2
3. Development of forest recreational areas	2.0
4. Construction of tourist hotels - additional 12,763 rooms	15.3
5. Tourism personnel, training, research and development	0.1
6. Boosting international tourism publicity	1.8

Source:- Council for Economic Planning and Development

The problems facing Taiwan in its future development of Tourism are very much those that have presented difficulties in the past. With over 50% of visitors coming from Japan and no short term likelihood of this being significantly reduced, Taiwan remains vulnerable to changes in the Japanese economy and efforts by other parts of the region to woo Japanese visitors. With China, in particular, continuing to encourage and provide for tourism this is likely to be drain on potential Taiwan visitors. At the same time diplomatic communication will remain limited and the obtaining of visas is likely to remain a problem in the short term at least. Other problems include the continuing shortage of direct international air links and limited representation of tourism in overseas countries. At present Taiwan has just four overseas tourist offices: three of which are in the USA.

On the more positive side, and apart from the government's planned investment projects, the popularity of Taiwan for the Japanese is arguably a good thing because the Japanese are disproportionately high spenders and this should help to consolidate Taiwan as one of the region's largest tourist money markets. At the same time the profile of Japanese visitors shows a heavy bias towards men so that scope exists for broadening the Japanese base by encouraging more women to visit.

Also on the positive side, it is likely that the Eighties will see more direct air links for Taiwan - in particular with European countries, where the Tourism Bureau see a potentially strong business/pleasure travel market as business and trade links grow. Already 1980 has seen the start of an air service between South Africa and Taiwan which is expected to give tourism a boost. As air links are formed so airline advertising should also help to promote visitor benefits in Taiwan.

A further factor which should encourage the tourism industry in Taiwan is the development of pleasure and business/pleasure travel by the local people in the countries of Asia Pacific. The ASEAN countries and its neighbours are showing solid economic growth and ever increasing trade and business dealings. With more money filtering through to the people at large, regional tourism is very much a growth area and Taiwan is well positioned to benefit from this. At the end of the Seventies and beginning of the Eighties - a time when rates of growth were declining for countries such as the USA, and Australia - the numbers of visitors from countries such as Hong Kong, Malaysia, Korea and the Philippines have been growing more satisfactorily. Even more to the point growth in tourism from these countries has been occurring with very little promotional assistance from Taiwan's tourism authorities.

MARKET FOR TOURISM OUT OF TAIWAN

A separate aspect of tourism as a market in Taiwan is its potential as a source of visitors to other countries. An important consideration here is Taiwan's overseas travel rules which have not long been tightened. For example, in 1979 Taiwan residents made up 9.3% of Hong Kong's visitors but in 1980 they accounted for only 5.4%. The percentage decline in numbers of visitors was 40%.

Some information on air travellers out of Taiwan is available from the 1981 SRH Taiwan Survey (op cit). The survey estimated that 6% of Taiwan's adults had travelled overseas by air in the previous 3 years:- half of these in the previous 12 months. These air travellers tended to be elderly and better-off. Unusually for the region as a whole, women were more likely to be recent air travellers than men.

In terms of personal income, 19% of those earning NT$20,000 or more a month had travelled overseas by air in the past 3 years. Urban dwellers and those in the North of the country were also more likely air travellers.

Of those who had travelled by air in the past 12 months, 53% gave pleasure as a reason for travelling and 47% some other reason. Of the pleasure travellers, 78% said they had travelled on a package tour while the rest had organised their own trip.

Although it is only an attitudinal predisposition 12% of all adults felt it likely that they would be travelling by air in the next 12 months. The profile of these likely travellers was younger than that of the actual travellers suggesting that there is a potential market for travel which has yet to emerge among younger middle aged adults.

Table 75 - Air travel by local residents

| | Total Adults | Male | Female | 15-19 | 20-24 | 25-29 | 30-44 | 45+ | Household income (NT$) | | |
									-19,999	20,000-29,999	30,000
('000s)	10,497	5,477	5,020	1,377	1,668	1,510	3,156	2,787	4,642	3,779	2,052
	%	%	%	%	%	%	%	%	%	%	%
Travelled by air outside Taiwan in											
- past 3 years	6	6	6	*	2	5	7	11	2	8	12
- past 12 months	3	2	4	*	1	3	4	4	1	3	6

Source:-   SRH Taiwan Survey - 1981

7 Financial markets

FINANCIAL SYSTEM

Taiwan's **monetary** institutions include the following:- the Central Bank of China, domestic banks, local branches of foreign banks, medium business banks (originally mutual savings and loans companies merged in 1979 to be able to provide more financial assistance to medium business enterprises), credit co-operative associations, credit departments of farmers and fishery associations. The total assets of these monetary institutions is in excess of 90 per cent of the assets of all financial institutions. The other financial institutions are the investment and trust companies, the postal savings system, insurance companies and bills finance companies.

The Central Bank of China is the government bank. As an agency of the Executive Yuan, it controls the financial system. The domestic banks include the so-called commercial and specialised banks, most of which have savings departments. There is also the Export-Import Bank - similar to the USA Eximbank - which is an independent corporate agency whose main function is to help finance export trade.

The postal savings system accepts both time and savings deposits, most of which are redeposited with the Central Bank of China. At the end of 1980 the postal savings system had 13.0% (NT$125 billion) of the deposits of all financial institutions.

Apart from the monetary institutions listed above none of the other financial institutions are permitted to accept deposits from the public. Trust, investment and insurance companies may take trust funds and insurance premiums. The bills finance companies assist clients in issuing short term bills and notes by creating a primary market (although they also operate in the secondary market by helping to promote bills and notes).

Table 76 - Number of financial institutions

End of Year	Total	Central Bank of China	Bank of Taiwan			Specialized and Commercial Banks			Credit Co-oper-ative Assoc-iations	Mutual Loans and Savings Co	Credit Depart-ment of Farmers Asso-iations	Postal Savings System
			Sub-total	Head Office	Branch Office	Sub-total	Head Office	Branch Office				
1970	879	1	39	1	38	346	12	334	83	114	295	1
1971	904	1	42	1	41	370	12	358	78	118	294	1
1972	922	1	44	1	43	385	12	373	77	122	292	1
1973	932	1	46	1	45	393	12	381	76	125	290	1
1974	956	1	48	1	47	407	12	395	76	132	291	1
1975	974	1	49	1	48	421	13	408	74	138	290	1
1976	983	1	50	1	49	480	14	466	75	88	288	1
1977	988	1	50	1	49	496	14	482	75	91	274	1
1978	1,033	1	53	1	52	616	19	597	75	9	278	1
1979	1,042	1	53	1	52	634	22	612	75	-	278	1
1980	1,056	1	53	1	52	647	23	624	75	-	279	1

Source:-   Central Bank of China

CURRENCY AND FOREIGN EXCHANGE

The monetary unit is the New Taiwan dollar which is circulated in coins of 1 and 5 dollars and notes of 10, 50, 100, 500 and 1000 dollars.

At the beginning of 1979 a foreign exchange market was established which adopted a mobile rate of exchange and a limited forward money exchange market to replace the system of pegging the New Taiwan dollar to US currency. A number of appointed banks representatives together with a representative of the Central Bank of China fix the lower and upper limits of the spot rate for buying and selling US dollars on a daily basis.

The general policy of recent years has been to hold the exchange rate low as an aid to Taiwan's export competitiveness. From February 1973 to July 1978 the NT dollar was pegged at 38 to the US dollar. Thereafter the Taiwan currency was revalued to 36 to the US dollar as a result of the generally weakening US currency, Taiwan's strengthening trade and current accounts, and economic growth backed by increased industrial output.

However, the end of the Seventies and the beginning of the Eighties saw a rapid increase in oil prices and a much strengthened US dollar backed by high US interest rates. These factors in turn had a serious effect on Taiwan's trade balance and slowed industrial production and resulted in an August 1981 devaluation of the Taiwan currency by 4.8% taking it back to its 1973-78 level.

Foreign exchange reserves have grown steadily through the Seventies with a generally favourable trade balance. At the end of 1980 the amount was in excess of US$7.0 billion.

Table 77 - Principal financial indicators

End of Year	Money Supply	Deposits	Loans & Discounts	Reserve Money	Rediscount Rate Percentage Per Annum
Amount (NT$ million)					
1970	32,035	101,237	94,389	20,978	9.80
1971	39,980	123,196	115,469	27,262	9.25
1972	55,126	163,096	142,758	37,605	8.50
1973	82,310	222,180	214,545	48,600	10.75
1974	88,079	272,822	302,251	65,185	12.00
1975	111,780	346,899	391,008	75,557	10.75
1976	137,560	433,586	450,758	100,168	9.50
1977	177,575	552,021	545,259	123,384	8.25
1978	238,079	735,893	693,647	164,941	8.25
1979	254,703	819,984	806,171	168,433	11.00
1980	305,444	960,026	1,021,339	196,470	11.00

Source:-   Central Bank of China

MONEY SUPPLY

Although money supply is generally related to economic growth, in 1980 money supply grew at 19.9% against 7.0% in 1979 while economic growth was down from 8.1% in 1979 to 6.7% in real terms in 1980. The main reasons for this situation were world price increases together with higher US dollar interest rates which led to a demand for capital in Taiwan, accelerated a investment in public works and anticipated local price inflation which led to increased consumer spending. The situation has led to a revision of banking regulations allowing more flexibility for interest rate adjustments.

Table 78 - Money supply

	1976	1977	1978	1979	1980
Net currency (A)	47,674	60,573	78,550	88,333	110,432
Net deposit money(B)	89,886	117,002	159,529	166,370	195,012
Money supply(C=A+B)	137,560	177,575	238,079	254,703	305,444

Source:-   Central Bank of China

LOANS AND DEPOSITS

Total deposits of all financial institutions reached NT$960,026m by the end of 1980 of which 58.4% were the deposits of banks. A breakdown of bank deposits at the end of 1980 shows that 39.9% were savings deposits, 21.6% time deposits and 12.8% checking accounts. The Seventies has generally seen the strongest growth rate for time deposits while the proportion of savings deposits declined.

Table 79 - Deposits of all banks by account

End of Year	Total	Checking Accounts	Passbook Deposits	Time Deposits	Savings Deposits	Government Deposits	Foreign Currency Deposits
Amount (NT$ million)							
1970	62,375	8,401	6,343	8,707	27,241	10,125	1,558
1971	76,288	11,155	8,036	10,242	36,579	9,078	1,198
1972	103,749	15,169	12,510	14,305	48,942	11,571	1,252
1973	139,133	23,148	17,088	16,939	58,991	21,374	1,593
1974	167,326	23,924	18,538	21,219	80,663	21,492	1,490
1975	217,557	32,221	24,443	42,610	87,165	29,278	1,840
1976	272,534	37,442	31,444	82,269	82,229	36,471	2,679
1977	335,949	47,370	40,198	108,791	100,452	36,795	2,343
1978	440,231	70,465	45,109	122,592	147,676	52,339	2,050
1979	474,061	71,994	48,138	103,845	181,749	65,575	2,760
1980	560,719	71,937	66,240	121,207	223,514	74,558	3,263

Source:-   Central Bank of China

Total loans and discounts for all financial institutions stood at NT$1,021,339 at the end of 1980 of which 67.9% were loans and discounts of banks. Private enterprises took 50.9% of bank loans and discounts with public enterprises taking 24.4%. Most of the remaining loans were to private individuals.

Table 80 - Loans and discounts of all banks by borrower

End of Year	Total	Government	Public Enterprises	Private Enterprises	Individuals & All Others
Amount (NT$ million)					
1970	68,840	3,306	12,148	45,401	7,985
1971	86,135	3,671	16,086	55,239	11,139
1972	104,599	3,914	18,093	69,967	12,625
1973	151,514	3,573	22,244	104,709	20,988
1974	214,759	3,871	39,497	152,154	19,237
1975	284,507	5,094	57,568	193,339	28,506
1976	317,704	6,647	66,130	208,476	36,451
1977	375,892	8,398	79,226	231,274	56,994
1978	470,186	12,590	86,440	284,211	86,945
1979	544,650	13,088	112,119	304,285	115,158
1980	693,599	14,480	169,069	352,948	157,102

Source:- Central Bank of China

Of the other main financial institutions the postal savings system had 13.0% of all deposits of financial institutions and credit co-operative associations had 11.1% at the end of 1980. In both cases deposits had increased more than ten times between the end of 1970 and the end of 1980.

Table 81 - Deposits of other main financial institutions

End of Year	Total	Credit Co-operative Associations	Medium Business Banks	Credit Departments of Farmers' Associations	Postal Savings System
Unit: NT$ million					
1970	28,338	9,947	4,975	4,723	8,693
1971	36,639	12,927	5,858	6,038	11,816
1972	45,765	16,368	6,844	7,660	14,983
1973	57,097	22,518	7,115	9,718	17,746
1974	75,656	27,639	8,833	13,844	25,340
1975	97,734	35,421	11,255	16,968	34,090
1976	125,695	43,460	13,872	22,150	46,213
1977	179,475	58,716	20,700	32,118	67,941
1978	240,022	80,622	29,479	43,148	86,773
1979	274,390	89,391	35,312	48,948	100,739
1980	341,336	106,943	45,749	63,586	125,058

Source:-   Central Bank of China

Loans and discounts of the other main financial institutions were dominated at the end of 1980 by the credit co-operative associations with 7.8% of total loans and discounts in the financial system.

Table 82 - Loans and discounts of other main financial institutions

End of Year	Total	Credit Co-operative Associations	Medium Business Banks	Credit Departments of Farmers' Associations	Postal Savings System
Unit: NT$ million					
Loans & Discounts					
1970	15,190	6,548	4,398	4,169	75
1971	17,935	8,270	5,051	4,502	112
1972	21,197	10,020	5,767	5,254	156
1973	29,567	15,268	7,176	6,920	203
1974	34,320	17,106	9,109	7,859	246
1975	49,629	24,386	12,629	12,199	415
1976	62,420	29,765	15,302	16,473	880
1977	84,404	38,435	22,851	21,970	1,148
1978	121,809	56,539	32,789	31,400	1,081
1979	145,329	65,031	40,080	38,849	1,369
1980	178,852	79,222	48,292	49,587	1,751

Source:-   Central Bank of China

FINANCIAL MARKET DEVELOPMENTS

Although Taiwan has been expelled from the International Monetary Fund it is proving to be an ever more attractive banking centre for international banks. Despite the possibility of souring relations with Mainland China, Taiwan's economic growth rate and its expanding trade make it an attractive banking market. In addition its foreign reserves well in excess of its long term foreign debt and its low debt service ratio (6.0%) have helped to give Taiwan a very healthy credit risk rating.

There has been a rush of new banks in Taiwan in 1980 - largely European and not Japanese - which has put some pressure on available trained personnel. The Ministry of Finance is now preparing to limit the opening of new branches to two or three a year and has set a number of tough qualifying regulations including more than 10 years experience of doing business with Taiwan banks, and the making of at least US$60 million of medium and long term loans to Taiwan companies in each of three years prior to making an application.

There are a number of conditions in Taiwan which do not help foreign banks: for example a lack of a rediscounting facility with the Central Bank, branches may not take time deposits and a limit on loans that can be made in a foreign currency. However, at a time of planned trade expansion and with overseas finance required for Taiwan's industrial restructuring, foreign banks are still finding the market an attractive one.

For the period of Taiwan's Ten Year Economic Development Plan, total domestic investment requirements are projected at NT$6,110.8 billion. The planned sources of capital to meet these requirements are shown below.

Table 83 – Requirements and sources of capital for domestic investment in the Eighties

Unit: NT$billion at 1979 prices

| Item | 1979 | | 1989 | | Total | | |
	Amount	As % of GNP	Amount	As % of GNP	1980-1984	1985-1989	1980-1989
Investment requirements	**382.4**	**32.9**	**868.8**	**34.9**	**2,422.1**	**3,688.8**	**6,110.8**
Fixed investment	322.3	27.7	744.5	29.9	2,161.3	3,193.3	5,354.6
Private sector	180.8	15.5	400.2	16.1	1,138.5	1,719.7	2,858.2
Government and Government enterprises	141.5	12.2	344.3	13.8	1,022.8	1,473.7	2,496.5
Inventory investment	60.0	5.2	124.3	5.0	260.8	495.4	756.2
Sources of capital	**382.4**	**32.9**	**868.8**	**34.9**	**2,422.1**	**3,688.8**	**6,110.8**
National savings	380.6	32.7	864.3	34.7	2,433.8	3,679.3	6,113.1
Government savings	97.5	8.4	211.5	8.5	598.8	898.9	1,497.7
Savings by government enterprises	25.7	2.2	58.1	2.3	165.5	248.6	414.2
Private savings	165.0	14.2	355.8	14.3	1,040.7	1,527.2	2,567.9
Depreciation	92.4	7.9	239.1	9.6	628.6	1,004.6	1,633.4
Net foreign borrowing	1.7	0.2	4.5	0.2	-11.7	9.5	-2.2

Source:- Council for Economic Planning and Development

Table 84 – Assets and liabilities of all financial institutions

			(NT$ billion)
(End yr)	1978	1979	1980
Total assets	**1,116**	**1,280**	**1,532**
Foreign assets	316	337	359
Loans and discounts	694	806	1,021
Portfolio investments	84	107	113
Real estate	10	12	17
Cash	13	17	22
Total liabilities	**1,116**	**1,280**	**1,532**
Foreign	112	135	163
Currency issued	90	102	129
Checking accounts	84	87	90
Passbook deposits	75	80	105
Time deposits	145	122	143
Savings deposits	322	393	488
Foreign currency deposits	2	3	4
Govt deposits	106	134	129
Other	180	224	281

Source:-   Central Bank of China

8 Industrial markets

INDUSTRIAL DEVELOPMENT

Bearing in mind that prior to 1950 Taiwan had virtually no industry at all with the main exception of sugar production, the development of its industry has been dramatic.

In the early years, food, textiles and building materials were given priority to cut down on costly imports. The Sixties saw industrial development aimed at export expansion with growth in particular in electrical appliances and the beginnings of a petrochemical industry. The Seventies brought an infrastructural development and the growth of heavy industrial products. The end of the Seventies and now the Eighties have seen the beginning of a planned move towards higher technology industries, such as electronics and machinery.

In 1980 industry's contribution to Net Domestic Product was 45.67% and 91% of Taiwan's total exports were manufactured goods. The industrial origin of Gross Domestic Product is shown below.

Table 85 - Industrial origin of GDPs

	1980 %
Total GDP	100.0
Agriculture	7.7
Mining	1.2
Manufacturing	41.8
Utilities	2.8
Construction	6.4
Transportation	6.3
Wholesale/retail trade	13.1
Other services	20.7

Source:-   DGBAS

The government has interfered minimally with the private sector but has taken on the development of certain industries with monopoly potential and has been responsible for ensuring a sound base and infrastructure. Government enterprises which come under the supervision of the Ministry of Economic Affairs include: the Taiwan Power Company, The Chinese Petroleum Corporation, The China Petrochemical Development Corporation, The China Steel Corporation, The China Shipbuilding Corporation, The Taiwan Fertilizer Company, The Taiwan Sugar Corporation, The Taiwan Machinery Manufacturing Corporation, The Taiwan Alkali Company, Chung-tai Chemical Industries Corporation, The Taiwan Metal Mining Corporation, The Taiwan Aluminium Corporation, The China Phosphate Industries Corporation and the BES Engineering Corporation.

When President Chiang took over the administrative leadership in 1972 as Prime Minister it was clear that certain planned industrial activity was needed in terms of communications, transport and base products if Taiwan's economic momentum was to be maintained. 10 major projects were instigated - six transport related, three for heavy and chemical industries and one for the construction of nuclear power plants. These were successfully completed early in 1980 and 12 new projects have been implemented and are due for completion by the mid 1980s.

The 12 projects are:-

- Around-the-island railroad
- New cross-island highways
- Kaoping region traffic improvement
- China Steel expansion
- Construction of two more nuclear power plants
- Taichung harbour expansion
- New towns and housing project
- Regional drainage
- Dike and levee construction
- Pingtung-Oluanpi highway widening
- Farm mechanisation
- Cultural centres

US$5.7 billion has been budgeted for these twelve projects.

The heavy industry sector has been particularly successful in the latter part of the Seventies. The production of heavy industry grew by 94.2% in the period 1976-1980. The steel industry has been built up gradually with first phase construction beginning in 1974 and second phase completion scheduled for 1982 (which will give an annual production of 3.25 million tonnes). The result has been a minimum of excess capacity (and more recently the plant has been exceeding capacity). The steel mill in turn boosted ship-building, which has also developed cautiously but steadily, and Taiwan now has its sights on the development of an automobile industry. A new automobile plant was in the pipeline with a 1988 production target of 200,000 units.

At the same time there has been solid expansion in light industry creating an increased demand for raw materials, intermediates, semi-finished products and components and parts all of which have created demand for heavy and chemical industries.

PRODUCTION STATISTICS

The general index of industrial production increased by 66.1% between 1976 and 1980. The average annual rate of increase for the Sixties was 15.8% and for the Seventies 15.3%. In 1980 industrial growth was 7.7%.

Private industry has become more important in industrial production over the last twenty years. In 1980 the private sector accounted for 80% of industrial production, compared with 52% in 1960. Growth rates for a number of selected manufactured products can be seen through the indices below.

Table 86 – Manufacturing indices for selected products by year

	1977	1978	1976=100 1979	1980
Manufacturing	112.9	142.6	153.7	165.2
Beverage & tobacco	115.7	137.8	136.2	132.2
Textile	105.0	117.0	117.3	131.9
Wearing apparel	105.7	131.9	140.9	173.8
Leather	121.6	176.0	250.0	244.8
Lumber & furniture	100.1	127.0	119.4	97.1
Paper & printing	111.3	141.9	167.3	175.2
Chemical materials	129.1	165.3	189.1	201.2
Chemical products	111.4	132.3	150.1	163.9
Petroleum & coal products	114.5	138.5	150.8	211.0
Rubber products	106.4	123.0	132.8	142.5
Plastic products	85.5	106.6	142.4	146.7
Non-metallic mineral products	113.9	125.9	126.3	141.2
Basic metals	124.6	177.0	198.5	188.6
Metal products	114.0	138.3	151.4	175.2
Machinery	110.8	136.4	150.2	138.2
Electrical machinery and appliances	116.3	172.9	174.4	193.0
Transport equipment	138.1	182.3	218.3	237.2
Precision instruments	258.7	322.7	250.6	276.6

Source:-   Industry of Free China

In terms of individual products the Seventies (1971-80) have seen particularly strong annual growth in production for such products as machine tools (31%), electric meters (28%), electric fans (20%), steel bars (21%), TV sets (17%), PVC (16%), sewing machines (13%), refined oil (13%) and cement (12%).

Table 87 - Output of principal industrial products by year

Item	Unit	1971	1978	1979	1980
Electric power	million kwh	15,171	34,432	37,897	40,814
Coal	000 m.t.	4,096	2,883	2,719	2,573
Refined sugar	000 m.t.	733	782	872	728
Canned pineapples	000 c/s	4,459	1,265	1,626	1,762
Canned asparagus	000 c/s	4,135	3,423	3,698	4,508
Canned mushrooms	000 c/s	2,893	4,346	3,319	2,862
Cotton yarns	000 m.t.	110	131	158	171
Cotton fabric	million m	625	766	754	807
PVC	000 m.t.	127	388	407	454
Polyester fibres	000 m.t.	13	157	172	192
Crude petroleum	000 kl.	125	246	230	211
Plywood	million m^2	316	451	445	356
Pulp & paper	000 m.t.	240	608	709	768
Sheet glass	000 c/s	1,772	2,833	3,239	3,633
Cement	000 m.t.	5,288	11,460	11,897	14,062
Sewing machines	000 set	787	2,007	2,076	2,193
Steel rods & bars	000 m.t.	501	1,874	2,114	1,966
Ship building	000 D.W.T.	279	431	382	572
Motorcycles	000 set	166	639	746	708
Television sets	000 set	1,891	7,046	5,870	5,770
Sound recorders	000 set	687	6,020	8,475	11,146
Household refrigerators	000 set	204	524	513	414
Aluminium ingots	000 m.t.	26	50	56	64
Alcoholic beverages	000 hl.	1,858	,m829	4,220	4,366
Cigarettes	million	16,604	24,025	24,835	35,834
Caustic soda	000 m.t.	135	362	420	400
Soda ash	000 m.t.	52	77	81	93
Pig iron	000 m.t.	108	316	325	272
Machine tools	000 unit	13	343	414	338
Electric fans	000 set	563	1,898	2,537	2,978
Watthour meters	000 piece	665	7,496	8,615	6,676

Source:-   Industry of Free China

At the end of 1980 the number of factories registered in Taiwan stood at 55,421 of which the largest single category was chemicals with 11,936 factories followed by machinery and tools with 11,220.   By comparison with 1975 the number of registered factories had grown by 35.2% the equivalent of 5.9% per annum.

Table 88 - Number of factories registered by year

	1976	1977	1978	1979	1980
Total	**43,809**	**47,704**	**52,849**	**59,449**	**55,421**
Food	6,749	6,991	7,290	7,887	7,177
Textiles	4,607	5,117	6,087	6,486	6,106
Chemicals	9,574	10,319	11,440	12,807	11,936
Saw mill and wood products	3,942	4,249	4,669	5,136	4,846
Ceramics	2,398	2,620	2,854	3,152	3,064
Metals	5,398	5,991	6,668	7,685	7,464
Machinery and tools	7,105	7,935	9,647	11,778	11,220
Printing and book binding	1,003	1,099	1,216	1,378	1,225
Others	3,033	3,383	2,978	3,140	2,383

Source:-   Provincial Department of Reconstruction

To facilitate the acquisition of land for industrial purposes, the government has designated 12 sites - in suitable areas for communication and labour - as industrial land and more sites are being added. In addition 42 industrial parks have been developed since 1963, all with good services and communications, in which land is sold to investors at reasonable prices.

The Government has also established three export processing zones which in effect are a combination of a free port and an industrial park and offer tax benefits as well as all relevant industrial facilities. These zones are located at Kaohsiung, Taichung and Nantze. At January 1980 investment by foreigners and Overseas Chinese in the three zones stood at 304 factories with an investment total of US$284 million.

With industrial emphasis being moved towards high technology industries, Taiwan has set up a specialised science-based industrial park at Hsinchu - about 70 kilometres south of Taipei - where several science and technology institutes are based. The Hsinchu Park has been established to take new factories in the following lines:
-    digital and linear electronics
-    precision instruments, precision machinery and components
-    materials science
-    consulting and service industries
-    energy and aeronautical industries

Apart from the nearby pool of technical expertise, enterprises operating at Hsinchu enjoy tax holidays, free remittance of capital out of Taiwan and guarantees against acquisition or nationalisation.

LEADING PRIVATE COMPANIES

According to a survey by the China Credit Information Service the top 500 private firms had an average increase in sales of 17.2% in 1980. The two leading companies were in plastics followed by a motor car company and the major electrical appliance and electronics manufacturer. The most profitable industries were cement, paper and pulp, cable and wire and pharmaceutical. The ten largest private manufacturers are shown below.

Table 89 - Ten largest private industrial corporations

Rank '80	'79	Company	Sales NT$ Million	Assets NT$ Million	Rank '80	'79	Employees Person	Rank '80	'79	Return on Sales %	Rank '80	'79
1	1	Nan Ya Plastics	20,723	18,659	2	1	9,799	4	3	4.66	168	139
2	2	Formosa Plastics	17,120	16,165	4	4	5,451	7	7	8.13	83	90
3	3	Yue Loong Motor	14,749	12,589	6	7	3,008	15	17	6.06	115	138
4	4	Tatung Co	14,289	17,956	3	2	15,000	1	1	3.15	218	234
5	5	Formosa Chemicals & Fibre	12,712	19,801	1	3	10,448	3	4	11.22	36	24
6	7	Taiwan Cement	11,499	10,301	7	8	2,729	17	18	10.52	43	37
7	6	Far Eastern Textile	10,645	15,501	5	5	12,012	2	2	3.11	220	103
8	8	Matsushita Electric (Taiwan)	8,003	4,229	23	17	4,500	10	9	7.04	97	120
9	10	Ford Lio Ho Motor	7,961	1,856	71	31	2,390	20	26	3.75	190	253
10	9	Sampo Corporation	7,597	6,026	11	12	5,300	8	10	5.06	154	171

Source:-   China Credit Information Service

INDUSTRIAL PLAN

Taiwan's Ten-Year Economic Development Plan projects a growth rate for the industrial sector as a whole in the Eighties at 10.0% per annum. The manufacturing sector is projected to grow at 10.3%.

Table 90 - Growth targets for individual sectors of the economy

| | | | | NT$ billion at 1979 prices | | |
| | | | | | Average Annual Growth Rate (%) | |
Sector	1979	1984	1989	'80-'84	'85-'89	'80-'89
Gross Domestic Product	**1,159.9**	**1,704.3**	**2,481.1**	**8.0**	**7.8**	**7.9**
Agriculture	**102.6**	**110.4**	**119.0**	**1.5**	**1.5**	**1.5**
Industry	**610.7**	**995.7**	**1,579.9**	**10.3**	**9.7**	**10.0**
Mining	12.6	15.8	19.4	4.5	4.2	4.4
Manufacturing	497.0	822.6	1,324.9	10.6	10.0	10.3
Construction	68.9	103.1	148.0	8.4	7.5	8.0
Electric power and other utilities	32.1	54.2	87.7	11.0	10.1	10.6
Services	**446.6**	**598.2**	**782.2**	**6.0**	**5.5**	**5.8**
Transportation and communications	71.2	103.2	144.8	7.7	7.0	7.4
Other services	375.4	494.9	637.4	5.7	5.2	5.4

Source:-   Council for Economic Planning and Development

Industry as a whole is planned to increase its share of GDP to 57.7% by 1989 with manufacturing taking 47.7%. The share of GDP taken by agriculture and mining will fall under the present plan.

Table 91 - Projected industrial structure

| | | % at current prices | |
	1979	1984	1989
Gross Domestic Product	**100.0**	**100.0**	**100.0**
Agriculture	8.9	7.0	5.5
Industry	52.6	55.7	57.7
- Mining	1.1	0.9	0.7
- Manufacturing	42.8	45.7	47.7
- Construction	5.9	6.0	6.0
- Electric power and other utilities	2.8	3.1	3.3
Services	38.5	37.3	36.8
- Transport and communication	6.1	6.1	6.1
- Others	32.4	31.2	30.7

Source:-   Council for Economic Planning and Development

The following is a summary of the basic policies designed to produce the planned growth in the manufacturing sector.

1. Setting up technology intensive industries with high value added and a relatively low energy co-efficient.

2. Orienting the development of capital intensive industries towards domestic industrial requirements.

3. Accelerating industrial modernisation to increase productivity.

4. Accelerating the introduction of advanced technology.

5. Actively promoting the use of computers with a view to increased efficiency.

6. Promoting interface between military, public and private enterprises to increase self-sufficiency in defence.

7. Actively assisting small and medium sized enterprises with growth potential.

8. Promoting the improvement of production equipment to save energy.

A number of measures have been laid down to help realise these objectives in the areas of taxation, foreign trade and technology. Financing is not seen as a problem area with Taiwan's solid credit rating likely to be an encouragement for foreign loans. For example, foreign capital is expected to absorb 20% of the total cost of the 12 major government projects for the Eighties.

In 1979 33.1% of Taiwan's industrial value added came from the metal manufacturing industries (with transportation equipment taking 7.3%). By 1989 value added by the metal industries is planned to grow to 46.6% of total value added (with transportation equipment taking 10.1%) Despite the planned move to higher technology industries, the textiles sector will still be the largest individual contributor to value added in 1989 with a planned 10.6% (having accounted for 14.1% in 1979). In terms of growth rate in value added textiles has the lowest planned rate for 1980-89 at 4.8% per annum. The highest rates of growth are forecast for machinery and telecommunications equipment (16.7% and 14.7% respectively).

Table 92 - Growth rates and structural changes planned for manufacturing industries

Unit: NT$ million at 1979 prices

Industry	Value Added						Average Annual Growth Rate %		
	1979		1984		1989				
	Amount	Percentage	Amount	Percentage	Amount	Percentage	1980-1984	1985-1989	1980-1989
Total	**496,998**	**100.0**	**822,599**	**100.0**	**1,324,899**	**100.0**	**10.6**	**10.0**	**10.3**
Chemical	129,644	26.1	198,271	24.1	285,507	21.5	8.9	7.6	8.2
Petroleum products	23,896	4.8	34,082	4.1	48,892	3.7	7.4	7.5	7.4
Petrochemical intermediates	9,466	1.9	16,651	2.0	23,886	1.8	12.0	7.5	9.7
Synthetic fibre	19,488	3.9	30,482	3.7	44,134	3.3	9.4	7.7	8.5
Plastic raw material	7,361	1.5	13,537	1.6	20,335	1.5	13.0	8.5	10.7
Plastic products	24,464	4.9	37,569	4.6	51,444	3.9	9.0	6.5	7.7
Other chemicals	44,969	9.0	65,950	8.0	96,816	7.3	8.0	8.0	8.0
Metal	164,753	33.1	326,014	39.6	617,951	46.6	14.7	13.6	14.1
Iron & steel	17,823	3.6	34,252	4.2	61,613	4.7	14.0	12.5	13.2
Other metals & metal products	28,491	5.7	56,950	6.9	107,054	8.1	14.9	13.5	14.2
General machinery	18,339	3.7	41,876	5.1	85,870	6.5	18.0	15.4	16.7
Household electric appliances	12,012	2.4	21,318	2.6	35,708	2.7	12.2	10.9	11.5
Telecommunication equipment	30,276	6.1	60,782	7.4	119,358	9.0	15.0	14.4	14.7
Electrical machinery and appliances	21,734	4.4	39,967	4.9	75,130	5.7	13.0	13.5	13.2
Transportation equipment	36,078	7.3	70,869	8.6	133,218	10.1	14.5	13.5	14.0
Others	202,601	40.8	298,314	36.3	421,441	31.8	8.1	7.2	7.6
Food	68,379	13.8	89,623	10.9	109,041	8.2	5.6	4.0	4.8
Textiles	70,195	14.1	102,945	12.5	140,965	10.6	8.0	6.5	7.2
Wood and wood products	15,806	3.2	20,135	2.4	25,089	1.9	5.0	4.5	4.7
Non-metallic mineral products	21,011	4.2	33,776	4.1	53,107	4.0	10.0	9.5	9.7
Other manufacturing	27,210	5.5	51,835	6.3	93,239	7.0	13.8	12.5	13.1

Source:- Council for Economic Planning and Development

The following production targets have been set for Taiwan's major industrial goods.

Table 93 - Production targets for major industrial products

Industry	Product	Unit	1979	1980	1984	1986	1989	1980-1989 Annual Growth Rate (%)
Steel	(Crude steel	000 m.t.	3,880	4,040	6,650	9,070	11,370	11.4
	(Bars	000 m.t.	1,800	1,950	2,600	2,800	3,200	5.9
	(Plates	000 m.t.	480	520	1,600	1,800	2,500	17.9
Other metal products	(Aluminium ingots	000 m.t.	60	70	100	120	140	8.8
	(Piping	000 m.t.	260	270	330	380	430	5.2
Machinery	(Industrial machinery	NT$ billion	31	35	57	78	125	15.0
	(Lathes	000 sets	20	24	40	60	80	14.9
Electrical machinery & appliances	(Motors	000 sets	1,600	1,970	3,670	4,850	7,380	16.5
	(Wires & cables	000 m.t.	170	180	410	560	880	17.9
	(Refrigerators	000 sets	530	570	920	1,110	1,480	10.8
	(Air conditioners	000 sets	260	220	760	1,000	1,520	19.3
Electronics	(Calculators	000 sets	6,770	6,420	7,520	9,420	13,320	7.0
	(Television	000 sets	6,930	7,780	7,500	8,260	9,500	3.2
Transportation equipment	(Automobiles	000 units	100	120	210	280	420	15.4
	(Motorcycles	000 units	620	650	1,090	1,340	1,830	11.4
	(Ships	000 gross tons	450	470	550	660	1,000	8.3
Petrochemicals	(Ethylene	000 m.t.	400	420	760	780	1,080	10.4
	(Styrene	000 m.t.	80	90	180	200	300	14.1
	(Acrylonitrile	000 m.t.	90	100	120	130	200	8.3
Synthetic fibres	(Polyamide	000 m.t.	100	80	120	130	150	4.1
	(Polyester	000 m.t.	320	320	460	540	650	7.3
	(Acrylic	000 m.t.	90	90	190	240	310	13.2
Plastics	(Low density polyethylene	000 m.t.	150	160	200	210	230	4.4
	(Polystyrene	000 m.t.	60	70	200	240	300	17.5
	(Polyvinyl chloride	000 m.t.	410	470	600	640	700	5.5
Petroleum products	(Motor gasoline	000 kl.	1,860	2,000	2,670	3,190	4,160	8.5
	(Fuel oil	000 kl.	9,980	11,300	14,280	17,050	22,260	8.4
Other chemical products	(Fertilizer	000 m.t.	420	440	470	480	490	1.5
	(Sulphuric acid	000 m.t.	860	900	1,200	1,480	1,900	8.2
	(Pulp	000 m.t.	530	580	850	1,030	1,350	9.8
Non-metallic mineral products	Cement	000 m.t.	11,600	14,200	20,370	24,650	32,810	11.0
Textiles	(Cotton yarn, cotton blended yarn	000 m.t.	310	330	440	490	580	6.5
	(Cotton fabrics, cotton blended fabrics	million m.	14,720	14,800	20,120	23,040	28,220	6.7
	(Garments	million dz.	67.5	69.1	103.0	116.0	138.0	7.4

Source:- Council for Economic Planning and Development

INVESTMENT

To facilitate investment in Taiwan, the Government has established the Industrial Development and Investment Centre under the Ministry of Economic Affairs. Its role is essentially one of trouble shooting and information provision.

The conditions for foreign investment have improved in recent years so that for approved investments:

- foreign investors may have 100% of the enterprises they invest in.

- all net profits and interest earnings can be converted and remitted.

- after one year of business, investors may apply for repatriation of 20% of each year's total invested capital.

- there is protection against government expropriation or requisition for 20 years if foreign investment is 45% of the total registered capital.

- greater security for patents, trademarks and copyrights (an area in which Government is very conscious of serious problems in the past).

In addition there are a number of tax incentives including tax holidays, the deduction of research and development expenses from business income taxes, lower tax rates, accelerated depreciation of fixed assets as well as the exemption of customs duty on machinery and equipment imports.

While detailed lists of desirable investment areas are available from the IDIC, in broad terms the key industries to be promoted in the Eighties are, steel and steel alloys, electrical and non-electrical machinery, industrial electronics, automobile manufacturing, computers, information, high performance plastics.

The enactment of the Statute for Encouragement of Investment in 1960 was a major step in encouraging overseas investment. In 1960 the inflow of foreign and overseas Chinese capital stood at US$15 million and that rose to US$466 million in 1980 despite a temporary decline with the recession of the mid Seventies. Reinvestment of retained earnings has been a significant feature of this period and a physical indication of investors' confidence.

Over the period 1952-80 a total of US$2,718 million of investments were approved of which 35% were from overseas Chinese, 29% from the USA, 17% from Japan and 10% from Europe. During this period Japanese investments have been growing disproportionately. On the whole they have tended to invest smaller amounts in more projects as the following figures show. In 1980 Japan accounted for 35.4% of investment approvals from foreign nationals (against 26.1% for the entire period 1952-80).

Table 94 – Overseas investments in approvals

	Cases (1980)	Amount
Overseas Chinese	39	222,584
Private foreign	71	243,380
- USA	15	110,093
- Japan	35	86,081
- Europe	11	14,428
- Others	10	32,778

Source:-   IDIC

The continuing growth of investment in Taiwan since derecognition is a relevant sign that this has not had serious consequences for the country's economic development.

In the period to 1980 electronic and electric appliances has been the area to attract most investment from foreigners and overseas Chinese accounting for 30% of all approvals. The next largest investment areas have been non-metallic mineral products (12%) and chemicals (11%).

Table 95 - Overseas investment by sector (1952-80)

	Overseas Chinese		Foreign		Total	
	Cases	Amount	Cases	Amount	Cases	Amount
Agriculture and forestry	14	2,962	-	-	14	2,962
Fishery and animal husbandry industry	45	9,633	6	1,822	51	11,455
Mining	2	359	2	215	4	574
Food and beverage processing	86	36,913	42	19,315	128	56,228
Textile	64	57,985	30	33,582	94	91,567
Garment and footwear	118	21,811	62	16,076	180	37,887
Lumber and bamboo products	47	17,567	25	5,233	72	22,800
Pulp paper and products	29	11,194	12	4,732	41	16,181
Leather and fur products	24	7,422	18	2,991	42	10,413
Plastic and rubber products	120	22,126	86	44,742	206	66,868
Chemicals	74	26,806	161	283,741	235	310,547
Non-metallic minerals	90	282,052	55	47,018	145	329,070
Basic metals and metal products	77	15,480	179	161,141	256	176,621
Machinery equipment and instruments	38	12,157	108	151,437	146	163,594
Electronic and electric appliances	90	20,512	325	831,334	415	851,846
Construction	150	91,322	6	9,954	156	101,276
Trade	94	5,583	3	2,285	97	7,868
Banking and insurance	18	51,654	18	49,750	36	101,404
Transportation	57	39,048	6	7,837	63	46,885
Services	100	211,283	40	46,252	140	257,535
Others	138	20,563	78	34,259	216	54,822
Total	1,475	964,687	1,262	1,753,716	2,737	2,718,403

Source:-   Industrial Development and Investment Centre

Taiwan has also been encouraging technical co-operation projects either with or independent of foreign capital. By the end of 1980 1,461 cases of technology transfer from abroad had been approved. Japan took the largest share of licensing with 69.1% of the total while the USA took 20.3%. The electronic/-electric appliance sector had the largest share of licensing with 26.1% of the total.

MAJOR PROJECTS FOR THE EIGHTIES

Taiwan's Ten-Year Plan lists a number of large scale (NT$2 billion plus) investment projects for the Eighties which will be largely funded by government and government enterprises. The total requirement for 120 specified projects is NT$3,097 billion of which the largest share, 29.9%, is for electric power projects,   followed   by   social   development   projects,   25.6%,   and transport/communication projects, 24.6%. The agriculture projects have been listed in the chapter on Agricultural Markets. The industry and service projects are listed below.

Table 96 - Major investment projects - industry and services

Unit: NT$billion

Project	Requirement in 1980-1989
Basic transportation and communications development (29 projects)	**763.0**
(1) Railroads	**85.5**
1. Procurement of additional rolling stock for the Around-the Island Railroad	22.9
2. Construction of the Around-the-Island Railroad (widening of the eastern trunk line and construction of the South Link Railroad	17.9
3. Modernization, improvement, and expansion of rail-transport facilities	17.6
4. Conversion of level crossings in heavy traffic areas to overpass crossings	10.0
5. Improvement of railroads in the Taipei municipal area	6.7
6. Widening of the Ilan railroad	5.1
7. Double tracking of the Chunan-Changhwa railroad	3.3
8. Improvement of the Pingtung-Kaohsiung railroad	2.0
(2) Highways	**113.4**
1. Expansion and modernization of highway passenger and freight transport and city bus fleets	45.0
2. Elimination of highway bottlenecks	36.0
3. Building additional freeway-interchange access roads and widening and improving old ones	11.4
4. Asphalt surfacing of all highways	10.0
5. Construction of three cross-island highways	6.0
6. Widening of the Pingtung-Oluanpi highway	3.0
7. Kaoping region traffic improvement	2.0
(3) Harbours	**29.8**
1. Third-phase construction of Taichung Harbour	7.4
2. Construction of cross-harbour tunnel and fourth container terminal at Kaohsiung Harbour	7.4
3. Construction and improvement of wharves for coastal transport system	7.3
4. Second-phase construction of Suao Harbour	5.0
5. Fourth stage of Hualien Harbour expansion	2.7
(4) Maritime transportation	**113.4**
1. Merchant fleet expansion project	109.0
2. Procurement of ships for coastal transport system	4.4
(5) Civil aviation	**53.6**
1. Procurement of additional civil aircraft	50.0
2. Second-phase construction of Chiang Kai-shek International Airport	3.6
(6) Mass transit system	**60.0**
Development of rapid mass transit systems in Taipei and Kaohsiung metropolitan areas	60.0
(7) Telecommunications	**299.3**
1. Expansion of local telephone networks	247.6
2. Expansion of domestic toll communications facilities	29.4
3. Expansion of international telecommunications facilities	22.3

(8)	**Postal services**	**8.0**
	Acquisition of new postal buildings and mechanized processing equipment	8.0

Social Development (17 projects)   793.1

(1) Regional, urban, and housing development   698.5

1.	Construction of public housing	240.0
2.	Construction of city roads	192.2
3.	Urban land consolidation	49.5
4.	Expansion of city water supply system	45.2
5.	Construction of public facilities	42.9
6.	Development of new industrial zones	39.4
7.	Construction of sewerage systems	29.2
8.	Development of new towns	28.0
9.	Urban flood control	26.0
10.	Environmental improvement and pollution control	6.1

(2) Social welfare development   48.0

1.	Construction of cultural and social education facilities	25.9
2.	Improvement of public health	15.1
3.	Development of social welfare facilities	7.0

(3) Tourism   46.6

1.	Development of national parks	21.2
2.	Construction of tourist hotels	15.3
3.	Development of scenic areas	8.1
4.	Development of forest recreational areas	2.0

Electric power (29 projects)   925.5

(1) Transmission and distribution facilities   131.2

(2) Nuclear power plants   320.5

1.	Units 1 and 2 of fourth nuclear plant	75.8
2.	Units 3 and 4 of third nuclear plant	72.6
3.	Units 3 and 4 of second nuclear plant	55.0
4.	Units 1 and 2 of fifth nuclear plant	39.0
5.	Units 1 and 2 of third nuclear plant	38.6
6.	Units 3 and 4 of first nuclear plant	22.8
7.	Units 1 and 2 of second nuclear plant	16.7

(3) Thermal power plants   400.7

1.	Units 6,7 and 8 of Hsingta thermal plant	56.2
2.	Units 3,4 and 5 of Suao thermal plant	55.0
3.	Units 3,4 and 5 of Hsingta thermal plant	50.5
4.	Units 1 and 2 of Chungpu thermal plant	47.1
5.	Units 1 and 2 of Suao thermal plant	34.2
6.	Units 1 and 2 of Peipu for peaking thermal plant	30.6
7.	Units 1,2 and 3 of Tungkang thermal plant	27.2
8.	Units 6 and 7 of Suao thermal plant	24.0
9.	Units 3 and 4 of Chungpu thermal plant	24.0
10.	Units 1 and 2 of Hsingta thermal plant	14.8
11.	Units 1 and 2 of Kyanyin thermal plant	12.7
12.	Gas turbine generator of Tunghsiao thermal plant	12.0
13.	Unit 4 of Hsiehho thermal plant	10.1
14.	Unit 3 of Hsiehho thermal plant	2.3

(4) Hydroelectric power   73.1

1.	Minghu pump-storage power project	17.5
2.	Mingtan pump-storage power project	14.0
3.	Maan hydropower project	13.3
4.	Kuyuan hydropower project	9.4
5.	Hsipan hydropower project	7.0
6.	New Tienlun hydro turbine project	6.9
7.	Sungmao and Mukuachi hydropower project	5.0

Mining (2 projects)   18.8

1.	Development of offshore petroleum/gas resources	15.4
2.	Development of limestone and marble deposits	3.4

Manufacturing (25 projects)	**350.1**
(1) Basic metals	**204.7**

1.	Second-stage expansion of China Steel Corporation's integrated steel mill	160.0
2.	First-stage second-phase expansion of China Steel Corporation's integrated steel mill	40.9
3.	Zinc smelter	3.8

(2) Metal products	**22.0**

1.	Heavy industrial equipment manufacturing plant	9.3
2.	Modernization of machinery and transportation equipment	9.2
3.	Facilities for prime-mover manufacturing and the rolling of high-strength alloys	3.5

(3) Chemicals	**120.5**

1.	Construction of additional gas stations	20.8
2.	Construction of additional oil storage facilities	15.1
3.	Central Taiwan oil refinery	11.0
4.	Expansion of storage tank facilities	10.0
5.	Kaohsiung low-sulphur fuel oil refinery	9.0
6.	First-stage facility for LNG imports	7.9
7.	Fifth naptha cracking plant	7.6
8.	Taoyuan low-sulphur fuel oil refinery	6.0
9.	Taoyuan refinery, 2nd unit	4.9
10.	Phosphoric acid plant	4.9
11.	Expansion of transport facilities for petroleum products	4.6
12.	Fourth naptha cracking plant	4.1
13.	Expansion of oil pipeline network	3.4
14.	Second fluidized catalytic cracking & fifth reforming units	2.5
15.	Expansion of chlorine plant & supporting facilities	2.4
16.	Expansion of Chungtai Chemical Industries Corp. caprolactam plant at Toufen	2.2
17.	Gasification plant for residual oil and No. 3 sulphur plant	2.1
18.	N-paraffin and linear mono-olefin plant	2.0

(4) Food industry	**2.9**

Modernization of sugar manufacturing and expansion of related facilities.	2.9

Source:-   Council for Economic Planning and Development

9 Agricultural markets

Agriculture's share of Taiwan's economic growth has been declining through the Sixties and Seventies. The structure of Taiwan's economy has changed dramatically over this period with agriculture's contribution to GDP falling from 31% in 1960 to 8% in 1980. Meanwhile, industry's contribution rose from 24% in 1960 to 46% in 1980. By 1989 agriculture is expected to contribute only 5.5% to GDP.

Nevertheless, agricultural development has not been neglected and the index of production has increased from 142.6 in 1960 (1952=100) to 286.9 in 1980 - an average growth rate of 5.1% per annum. Taiwan is 85% self-sufficient in basic foodstuffs.

The essential problem for any growth in Taiwan's agricultural sector is the inhospitability of the terrain. The land is mainly mountainous. There are about 1.3 million hectares of level land which is just 36.4% of the total land area. 25% of the total land area is already under cultivation and over 60% of this has to be irrigated, so there is not much scope for expanding arable land.

There are just under 900,000 farm households with a farm population of 5.6 million - about 30% of the total population. In 1979 the average farm size was 1.04 hectares and the average farm family had 6.4 persons. As an indication of farmers increasing income, farmers' deposits rose from NT$128 million in 1952 to NT$53,191 million in 1979.

Table 97 - Agricultural production index by year

	1978	1979	1976=100 1980
General	102.1	107.5	106.4
- Crops	97.0	100.4	98.2
- Forestry	78.8	70.8	66.3
- Animal husbandry	118.6	131.5	131.6
- Fishery	112.6	122.6	125.8

Source:-   Council for Agricultural Planning and Development

HISTORICAL DEVELOPMENT

The end of the Forties and early Fifties saw a number of important land reforms in Taiwan. Prior to that time about 80% of the farm land was privately owned and the majority of that land was under tenancy. Tenants generally had a poor deal from landlords with heavy rents of 50 per cent or more of crop yield, usually payable well in advance and with a minimum of protection. Levels of agricultural production were very low.

Under Taiwan's land reform programme a number of measures were carried out. In 1949 limits were set for farm rentals and more protection given to tenants. In 1951 the Government started selling its own land to tenant farmers (in the period to 1964 210,000 tenant families had land transferred). In 1953, under the so-called 'Land to the Tiller' programme, private holdings were compulsorily purchased by the government and sold to incumbent tenants. 55% of all privately tenanted land was bought in this way and resold, bringing farm ownership in Taiwan up to 86%.

Since the early Fifties further measures have been taken for farm land consolidation. The main effects of these have been to improve irrigation and drainage, to provide more access roads, to introduce more mechanisation and better pest control, to provide uniform plots with clear boundaries and generally to improve farm management and farming community development. The government has also been active in the area of tax relief and preferential loans to farmers and in reducing fertiliser prices.

AGRICULTURAL PRODUCTION

Taiwan has just over 900,000 hectares of arable land of which about 60% is paddy fields and 40% dry land. Land suitable for rice cultivation has been fully utilised but production increases have been maintained through the Seventies by improved farming methods including the planting of higher yielding varieties and the better use of fertilisers. Rice is Taiwan's major agricultural product. However, in common with other agricultural products, rice production declined in 1980:- 4% down on the year before. Higher costs, unfavourable crop prices and poor weather were all contributing factors in reducing Taiwan's 1980 agricultural output by 1%.

Sweet potatoes and sugar cane are the other major crops. The former used to be the major pig feed in Taiwan but an increase in imported feed corn has reduced the need for sweet potatoes. In 1980 sweet potato production was down by 11.8%. Sugar is the main export crop but sugar cane output also declined in production in 1980 by 4.8%. Other useful export earners are pineapples, asparagus and mushrooms- for which Taiwan is the world's leading exporter - as well as bananas and citrus fruits.

Table 98 - Agricultural production (major products) by year

		Unit	1979	1980	% change
1.	**Farm crops**				
	Rice	000 m.t.	2,450	2,354	-3.9
	Sweet potatoes	000 m.t.	1,225	1,055	-13.9
	Soybeans	m.t.	31,782	25,934	-18.4
	Wheat	m.t.	2,521	2,839	12.6
	Peanuts	m.t.	85,881	86,127	0.3
	Refined sugar	m.t.	845,139	829,639	-1.8
	Tea	m.t.	27,055	24,479	-9.5
	Bananas	m.t.	226,769	214,323	-5.5
	Pineapples	m.t.	244,777	228,804	-6.5
	Citrus fruits	m.t.	398,828	374,381	-6.1
	Asparagus	m.t.	102,837	112,871	9.8
	Mushrooms	m.t.	103,426	76,159	-26.4
2.	**Livestock**				
	Hogs (slaughtered)	000 head	7,428	6,956	-6.3
	Cattle (slaughtered)	000 head	47	33	-30.6
	Chickens (slaughtered)	000 head	94,253	104,685	11.1
	Milk	m.t.	44,418	47,740	7.5
3.	**Fisheries**				
	Deep sea	m.t.	362,268	370,342	2.2
	Inshore	m.t.	350,801	358,207	2.1
	Coastal	m.t.	32,569	32,777	0.6
	Fish culture	m.t.	183,688	175,008	-4.7
4.	**Forestry**				
	Timber	m^3	654,165	582,663	-10.9

Source:-   Taiwan Fisheries Bureau, Taiwan Forestry Bureau, Ministry of
Economic Affairs, Provincial Department of Agriculture and Forestry

More than half of Taiwan is covered by forests - a total land area of almost 1.9 million hectares.   However much of the timber is of poor quality and inaccessible.   Measures taken to protect resources and for soil conservation have seen timber output decline and no increase is planned through the Eighties. There are still many wood processing plants in Taiwan which in 1980 together exported nearly US$1.1 billion of plywood, wood products and furniture.

Table 99 - Area of forest

	1980 (000 hectares)
Total	1,865
- Conifers	417
- Conifer/hardwood mix	157
- Hardwoods and bamboo	1,291

Source:-   Taiwan Forestry Bureau

In terms of livestock, the main categories are pigs and poultry. In 1980 667,000 metric tons of pigs were slaughtered - up by 4.0% on 1979, although cattle slaughtering fell by 21% as a result of a decrease in the cattle population and a rise in beef imports. Poultry are important in the domestic market with both chickens and ducks traditionally favoured meat. There is a growing dairy industry and it is of interest that the Chinese in Taiwan have a more favourable disposition to milk than Chinese in other countries which is believed to be due to a long period of Japanese influence on the island.

Table 100 -   Livestock production

End of	1979	1980	(number of head)
Cattle	142,829	133,813	
Pigs	5,417,706	4,820,201	
Goats	187,687	183,602	
Dairy cattle	11,280	11,045	
Chickens	38,941	41,394	
Ducks	9,995	9,928	

Source:-   Provincial Department of Agriculture and Forestry

The Seventies saw a steady increase in Taiwan's fishing industry with improved freezing facilities, expansion of the fleet, government loans and other technological advances. At the end of the decade, fishing limit impositions and high fuel costs affected the fishing industry and 1980 production declined by 11.3%. Fish products, nevertheless, still represent a useful export market for Taiwan valued at US$306.1 million in 1980 - an increase of 16.2% over 1979.

Japan is by far the main export market for Taiwan's fish products.

FARM MECHANISATION

In recent years the government has placed considerable emphasis on farm mechanisation to increase agricultural productivity. The main government action has been to provide low-interest loans to allow farmers to buy mechanical implements. Up until 1977 loans were offered at 70 per cent of the purchase cost, but this was seen as something of a disincentive, and from 1978 loans for the full amount have been offered. Under the revised loan scheme, annual purchasing by farmers is expected to be at the following levels - 9000-9500 power tillers, 500-650 tractors, 5000-8000 rice threshers, 1,800-4,000 combine harvesters, and 6000-7000 grain dryers.

Table 101 –   Production targets for major agricultural products

Item	Unit	1984	1986	1989	Average Annual Growth (%) 1980-1989
1. Farm crops					
Rice	000 m.t.	2,320	2,350	2,400	0.08
Sweet potatoes	000 m.t.	916	871	812	-4.18
Soybeans	000 m.t.	88	96	109	12.69
Corn	000 m.t.	286	335	403	14.07
Peanuts	000 m.t.	97	99	103	1.47
Refined sugar	m.t.	807	810	810	-0.42
Tea	000 m.t.	29	30	29	1.50
Tobacco	000 m.t.	21	24	28	3.42
Silkworm cocoons	m.t.	2,300	2,500	3,000	9.14
Bananas	000 m.t.	250	265	285	3.05
Pineapples	000 m.t.	179	180	183	-1.18
Citrus fruits	000 m.t.	478	492	509	2.86
Asparagus	000 m.t.	100	87	72	-3.42
Mushrooms	000 m.t.	88	83	70	-3.60
2. Livestock					
Hogs (slaughtered)	000 head	7,500	7,700	8,600	2.38
Cattle (slaughtered)	m.t.	4,800	4,900	5,000	0.41
Chickens (dressed)	000 birds	122,500	135,000	156,000	4.97
Milk	m.t.	137,000	165,800	220,660	17.23
3. Fisheries					
Deep-sea	000 m.t.	440	525	680	6.66
Inshore	000 m.t.	405	425	445	2.61
Coastal	000 m.t.	33	34	35	0.59
Fish culture	000 m.t.	257	289	340	6.16
4. Forestry					
Timber	000 m³	609	609	609	-1.52

Source:-   Council for Economic Planning and Development

Table 102 –   Farm ownership of mechanical implements

	End of 1979
Power tillers	84,254
Tractors	2,894
Rice transplanters	25,820
Combine harvesters	10,569
Grain dyers	25,032

Source:-   China Yearbook - 1980

FUTURE DEVELOPMENT

Taiwan's Ten-Year Economic Development Plan foresees an average annual growth rate of 1.5% for the agricultural sector. Within the sector as a whole, fisheries production is given the highest average annual growth rate at 3.8%, followed by livestock (2.8%), crops (0.4%), while timber output will decline by 1.2% per annum.

In terms of individual product categories the highest annual growth rates through the Eighties are planned for milk (17.2% per annum), corn (14.1%), soy beans (12.7%), silkworm cocoons (9.1%) and deep-sea fishing (6.7%).

The main measures to be taken to reach the specified production goals include the following:

- further land reform with more consolidation of holdings, enlarging the scale of operations and promoting mechanisation.

- an agricultural protection policy to guarantee prices.

- increased marketing control to raise farmers' income (relative per capita income of farm households is expected to rise from 64% in 1979 to 70% in 1989).

- the development of further (albeit limited) land resources and the planned allocation of water, and a general improvement in all agricultural production conditions.

- improving farmers' welfare.

- planned development of fish resources and further modernisation of the fishing industry.

Fixed investment in agriculture will total NT$267 billion through the Eighties - the equivalent of 5% of total fixed investment in agriculture, industry and services. 1.23 million people (14.9% of the labour force) are expected to be employed in the agricultural sector in 1989 - down from 1.38 million in 1979.

For the Eighties, the government has specified 18 major projects concerned with farm mechanisation and the agricultural infrastructure which will be largely funded by the government and government enterprises. These are listed below.

Table 103 –   Major investment projects - agriculture

	Unit: NT$ billion
Project	Requirement in 1980-1989
Farm mechanization and agricultural infrastructure (18 projects)	**246.3**
1. Agricultural mechanization	77.2
2. Construction of reservoirs	56.0
3. Construction of fishing boats	15.9
4. Reforestation	15.4
5. Strengthening and construction of river dikes and sea dikes	13.0
6. Construction of fishing harbours	9.7
7. Watershed protection, gully and flood control program	8.5
8. Development of shallow-sea fish culture	8.1
9. Construction and maintenance of industrial roads	7.0
10. Replacement of fishing boat equipment	6.0
11. Improvement of irrigation and drainage facilities	5.0
12. Rural community development	4.4
13. Improvement of regional drainage systems	4.4
14. Land consolidation	4.4
15. Slope land development and utilization program	4.1
16. Large-scale irrigation projects	2.7
17. Construction of forest roads and transportation facilities	2.3
18. Tidal land and riverbed land development	2.2

Source:-   Council for Economic Planning and Development

MINERAL RESOURCES

Taiwan's mineral resources are limited. Mining accounted for 1.1% of GDP in 1979 and by 1989 this is expected to decline to 0.7%. At the end of the Seventies only 1% of the labour force was engaged in mining. The country's principal resources are coal, natural gas, limestone, marble and dolomite.

Table 104 -   **Principal mineral reserves**

Ore	Locality	Unit	Reserves (end 1980)
Coal	Taipei, Keelung, Taoyuan, Hsinchu, Miaoli, Nantou, Chiayi	000 m.t.	205,300
Gold	Juifang, Chinkuashih (Taipei prefecture)	000 m.t.	6,582
Copper	Juifang, Chinkuashih (Taipei prefecture), Jemei (Hwalien	000 m.t.	12,565
Pyrites	Chihsingshan, Chinkuashih (Taipei prefecture), Tananao (Yilan), Tungmeng (Hwalien)	000 m.t.	1,814
Placer Magnetite	Chinshan, Tanshui (Taipei prefecture), Chuwei (Taoyuan), Chengkong (Taitung)	m.t.	133,000
Limonite	Taoyuan, Hsinchu, Taichung, Chihsingshan (Taipei Prefecture)	m.t.	984,000
Manganese	Simaoshan (Yilan)	m.t.	300,000
Ilmenite	Tainan, Chiayi, Hsinchu, Taoyuan, Taipei	m.t.	45,000
Zircon Ore	Tainan, Chiayi, Hsinchu	m.t.	24,000
Monazite	Tainan, Chiayi, Hsinchu	m.t.	90,000
Sulphur	Chihsingshan (Taipei prefecture), Chinshan, Peitou (Yangmingshan)	000 m.t.	2,405
Petroleum	Miaoli, Hsinchu, Taiwan	000 kl	2,008
Natural Gas	Miaoli, Hsinchu, Taiwan	Million m^3	27,423
Asbestos	Fengtien (Hwalien)	m.t.	67,800
Dolomite	Hwalien	000 m.t.	117,122
Marble	Yilan, Hwalien	Million mt	299,942
Talc	Yilan, Hwalien	000 m.t.	2,333

Source:-   Ministry of Economic Affairs

In its Ten-Year Plan the government is proposing further exploration for mineral resources with emphasis on those used as raw materials for basic industries. Fixed investment in the mining sector will average NT$4.1 billion per annum through the Eighties. Planned production levels are as shown below, with crude oil production growing fastest but from a small base.

Table 105 -   **Production targets for major mineral products**

Item	Unit	1980	1984	1986	1989	1980-89 Average Growth Rate (%)
Coal	000 m.t.	3,000	3,000	3,000	3,000	0.7
Crude oil	000 k.l.	240	245	345	1,140	16.9
Natural gas	mil.m^3	2,340	2,390	4,270	4,370	6.4
Limestone	000 m.t.	21,000	31,500	34,000	36,000	7.2

Source:- Council for Economic Planning and Development

10 External trade

OVERALL SITUATION

In the period since the beginning of the Fifties, Taiwan's external trade has expanded rapidly so that by the end of 1980 it was the 22nd largest trading nation in the world. By 1980 total trade stood at US$39.5 billion, having run at about one third of a billion through the Fifties. Taiwan's balance of payments has remained relatively strong despite a rapid increase in the oil bill at the end of the Seventies with the trade balance remaining in surplus for the second half of the decade. In 1980 the increase in cost and amount of oil imports led to a very much reduced trade surplus of US$77.5 million (after US$1,329.7 million in 1979). After service and transfer payments there was a current account deficit approaching one billion US dollars.

In 1980 Taiwan's exports grew by 23%, but this was largely a result of increased unit prices. In terms of quantity exports were only up by 10.7%. Adverse factors for exports were sluggish US demand, strengthening of the Taiwan currency against the Japanese Yen, a general deterioration in world trade and increased protectionism.

Imports were up by 33.6% in 1980. Apart from oil (imports up by 88.7% over 1979) contributing factors were higher unit costs, liberalisation of import controls and duties, and a sharp increase in imports from the US as a result of government efforts to narrow the trade gap.

Table 106 –   Taiwan's overall trade by year

Year	Total Trade	Exports	Imports		Surplus (+) or Deficit (–)
1968	1,692.5	789.2	903.3	(–)	114.1
1969	2,262.1	1,049.4	1,212.7	(–)	163.3
1970	2,952.2	1,428.3	1,523.9	(–)	95.6
1971	3,904.3	2,060.4	1,843.9	(+)	216.5
1972	5,501.6	2,988.1	2,513.5	(+)	474.6
1973	8,275.9	4,483.4	3,792.5	(+)	690.9
1974	12,604.8	5,639.0	6,965.8	(–)	1,326.8
1975	11,260.5	5,308.8	5,951.7	(–)	642.9
1976	15,765.2	8,166.3	7,598.9	(+)	567.4
1977	17,871.6	9,360.7	8,510.9	(+)	849.8
1978	23,714.0	12,687.1	11,026.9	(+)	1,660.2
1979	30,877.0	16,103.4	14,773.7	(+)	1,329.7
1980	39,543.7	19,810.6	19,733.1	(+)	77.5

Source:-   Customs Statistics of the R.O.C.

With its limited natural resources Taiwan needs to import large amounts of raw material and capital equipment. In 1980 agricultural and industrial raw materials accounted for 70.8% of Taiwan's total imports by comparison with 63.4% in 1970. Capital equipment took 23.4% of all imports and consumer goods 5.8%. Although Taiwan's markets for consumer goods have been growing with increased affluence among the people at large, the proportion of total imports accounted for by consumer goods has been steadily declining since 1977 (when they accounted for 7.8% of total imports).

Taiwan's export statistics show the steadily increasing domination of industrial products. In 1952, rice and sugar combined accounted for 74% of total exports and industrial goods accounted for just 8.1%. By 1970 industrial goods accounted for 80.3% of exports and in 1980 the figure stood at 90.8%. However in gross terms agricultural products, processed and unprocessed, have been growing steadily as exports and helping to bring prosperity to the rural areas.

COMMODITY IMPORTS

With the development of Taiwan's industry the need for crude petroleum has increased significantly. In 1980 it was by far the major import category with 20.8% (up from 14.7% in 1979). Machinery and tools, which was the leading import category of the Seventies up until 1977 when crude petroleum took over, was the second largest import category in 1980 with 11.6%. In order, the other leading categories were electrical machinery/apparatus and chemicals.

Table 107 –   **Commodity imports by year**

Unit   : US$ million

Commodities	1979 Amount	%	1980 Amount	%	Increases 1980 over 1979 Amount	%
Total	**14,773.7**	**100.0**	**19,773.1**	**100.0**	**4,959.4**	**33.6**
Major Primary Products	4,021.2	27.2	6,135.5	31.1	2,114.3	52.6
Crude petroleum	2,175.6	14.7	4,104.5	20.8	1,928.9	88.7
Lumber	632.7	4.3	633.5	3.2	0.8	0.1
Soya Bean	316.7	2.1	291.9	1.5	-24.8	-7.8
Maize	363.8	2.5	437.0	2.2	73.2	20.1
Wheat	191.2	1.3	208.0	1.1	16.8	8.8
Wool	53.5	0.4	59.8	0.3	6.3	11.8
Raw Cotton	287.7	1.9	400.8	2.0	113.1	39.3
Major Manufacturing Products	**8,815.2**	**59.7**	**11,201.9**	**56.6**	**2,386.7**	**27.1**
Electrical, machinery & apparatus	1,684.3	11.4	2,047.5	10.4	363.2	21.6
Metal products	128.9	0.9	146.6	0.7	17.7	13.7
Machinery	1,538.0	10.4	2,298.7	11.6	760.7	49.5
Iron & steel	1,017.5	6.9	1,342.4	6.8	324.9	31.9
Non-ferrous metal	461.8	3.1	621.2	3.1	159.4	34.5
Transportation equipment	1,176.1	8.0	1,233.2	6.2	57.1	4.9
Synthetic fibres	122.4	0.8	112.3	0.6	-10.1	8.3
Food, beverages & tobacco products	367.0	2.5	423.6	2.1	56.6	15.4
Chemicals	1,282.5	8.7	1,476.9	7.5	194.4	15.2
Plastics	231.4	1.6	247.5	1.3	16.1	7.0
Dyeing, tanning & colouring materials	110.8	0.7	121.7	0.6	10.9	9.8
Medical & pharmaceutical products	123.2	0.8	122.7	0.6	-0.5	-0.4
Pulp, paper & allied products	171.0	1.2	198.9	1.0	27.9	16.3
Refined petroleum products & fuel gas	264.1	1.8	638.2	3.2	374.1	141.7
Watches & clocks	136.2	0.9	170.5	0.9	34.3	25.2
Others	1,937.3	13.1	2,395.7	12.3	458.4	23.6

Source:- Customs Statistics of R.O.C.

Japan has been the main source of Taiwan's imports right through the Seventies and in 1980 Japan accounted for 27.1% of Taiwan's total imports. The USA accounted for 23.7% of imports to Taiwan in 1980 but this is expected to increase with Taiwan's efforts to balance its trade with the USA by taking in more imports from that country. West Germany and the United Kingdom are the main European import sources.

Table 108 –   **Sources of imports by year**

Unit: US$ million

Country	1976	1977	1978	1979	1980
Japan	2,451.5	2,643.0	3,678.1	4,561.4	5,353.2
U.S.A.	1,797.6	1,963.8	2,376.1	3,380.8	4,673.5
Kuwait	680.1	670.4	792.5	1,155.1	2,240.9
Saudi Arabia	409.3	489.2	648.6	864.8	1,418.9
Germany, Fed. Rep. of	352.2	276.9	411.9	635.6	722.3
Australia	182.6	216.5	322.0	454.0	539.6
Indonesia	201.3	313.6	319.7	452.2	539.6
United Kingdom	165.3	177.5	243.8	296.1	488.7
Malaysia	105.0	146.2	226.6	329.0	424.8
South Africa	98.5	88.2	144.9	214.7	266.1
Hong Kong	101.4	200.3	152.7	205.4	249.9
Import Total (Including Others)	7,598.9	8,510.9	11,026.9	14,733.7	19,773.1

Source:-   Customs Statistics of the R.O.C.

COMMODITY EXPORTS

Textile products have remained Taiwan's main export earner through the Seventies and in 1980 accounted for 24.2% of the country's total exports. Other major export items include electronic products (14.9% of 1980 exports), footwear (7.8%), wood products and furniture (5.8%), toys and sports goods (4.8%), and machinery (3.7%).

Table 109 –   **Commodity exports by year**

Unit : US$ million

Commodities	1979 Amount	%	1980 Amount	%	Increases 1980 over 1979 Amount	%
Total	**16,103.4**	**100.0**	**19,810.6**	**100.0**	**3,707.2**	**23.0**
Major Primary Products	365.8	2.2	424.2	2.1	58.4	16.0
Fishery Products	263.4	1.6	306.1	1.5	42.7	16.2
Farm products	102.4	0.6	118.1	0.6	15.7	15.3
Major manufacturing products	**14,099.5**	**87.4**	**17,315.4**	**87.4**	**3,215.9**	**22.8**
Textiles & articles thereof	947.1	5.9	1,144.6	5.8	197.5	20.9
Garment of textile fabric	1,797.7	11.2	2,215.9	11.2	418.2	23.3
Fibre, yarn line & fabric	806.8	5.0	841.4	4.2	34.6	4.3
Electrical machinery	486.0	3.0	685.8	3.5	199.8	41.1
Electronic products	2,336.8	14.5	2,946.8	14.9	610.0	26.1
Plywood, wood products and furniture	1,180.7	7.3	1,139.2	5.8	-41.5	-3.5
Metal products	695.7	4.3	869.5	4.4	173.8	25.0
Machinery	601.8	3.7	739.5	3.7	137.7	22.9
Iron & steel	536.4	3.3	337.8	1.7	-198.6	-37.0
Non-ferrous metal	47.3	0.3	57.4	0.3	10.1	21.4
Sugar & sugar preparations	87.6	0.5	232.2	1.2	145.2	166.9
Canned mushrooms	83.6	0.5	95.3	0.5	11.7	14.0
Canned asparagus	110.2	0.7	134.7	0.7	24.5	22.2
Canned & preserved foods	631.1	3.9	679.3	3.4	48.2	7.6
Transportation equipment	445.2	2.8	637.6	3.2	192.4	43.2
Refined petroleum products & fuel gas	275.8	1.7	289.9	1.5	14.1	5.1
Rubber products	132.6	0.8	198.9	1.0	66.3	50.0
Pulp, paper & allied products	86.4	0.5	121.5	0.6	35.1	40.6
Cement & cement products	14.6	0.1	25.5	0.1	10.9	74.7
Glass & glass products	86.9	0.5	108.7	0.5	21.8	25.1
Plastics	69.9	0.4	119.9	0.6	50.0	71.5
Plastic products	512.2	3.2	609.4	3.1	97.2	19.0
Footwear	985.4	6.1	1,547.7	7.8	562.3	57.1
Watches & clocks	141.5	0.9	177.5	0.9	36.0	25.4
Photoghraphic & optical goods	139.2	0.9	178.1	0.9	38.9	27.9
Potterware, chinaware and earthenware	143.4	0.9	220.9	1.1	77.5	54.0
Toys, fishing & hunting equipment, sporting goods	718.2	4.5	960.4	4.8	242.2	33.7
Others	1,638.1	10.4	2,071.0	10.5	432.9	26.4

Source:-   Customs Statistics of the R.O.C.

The USA, Japan and the EEC countries account for over 60 per cent of Taiwan's exports and Taiwan's success in exporting to these countries has brought demands for protectionist measures. This has led Taiwan to seek new markets to broaden its trade structure. There is now trading with Eastern Europe although more emphasis is being put on the newly industrialising countries of South America and Africa.

There have been trade difficulties for Taiwan as a result of current problems over the counterfeiting of trade and country of origin marks. The government is clearly conscious of this problem and the Board of Foreign Trade has promised prompt action in cancelling licences to manufacture and trade and in referring cases to courts.

Table 110 –   **Sources of exports by year**

Unit: US$ million

Country	1976	1977	1978	1979	1980
U.S.A.	3,038.7	3,636.3	5,010.4	5,652.2	6,760.3
Japan	1,094.7	1,120.0	1,570.3	2,248.6	2,173.4
Hong Kong	610.4	638.4	857.7	1,140.4	1,550.6
Germany, Fed. Rep. of	422.1	422.1	572.5	742.6	1,075.9
Australia	223.9	242.8	333.9	419.2	539.4
Canada	313.6	275.9	326.8	415.5	459.7
United Kingdom	162.9	271.9	322.6	406.0	472.7
Saudi Arabia	124.5	226.0	321.6	475.8	544.5
Indonesia	219.3	234.3	304.8	398.9	478.2
Singapore	213.6	232.8	296.1	422.3	545.2
Grand Total (Including Others)	8,166.3	9,360.7	12,687.1	16,103.4	19,810.6

Source:-   Customs Statistics of the R.O.C.

FUTURE TRADE DEVELOPMENT

Despite despondency in Taiwan over the USA's 1978 derecognition, the trade impact has been minimal and by acting as an incentive to Taiwan to increase its trade base it is now thought even to have done some good. Although only 22 countries - mainly from South America and the Middle East - have diplomatic relations with Taiwan, more than 150 maintain trade and other economic relations. Apart from developing trade with newly industrialised countries, Taiwan has developed stronger trade with Western Europe - 1980 trade stood at

US$4.9 billion about US$2 billion up on 1978.

However, the USA remains a vital trading partner for Taiwan. Not only does the USA still account for the largest share of Taiwan's total trade but Taiwan has a solid trade surplus in its favour. Total trade with the USA grew 17.6% in 1979 and 18.6% in 1980. Just prior to derecognition the USA granted a broad range of import duty concessions to Taiwan and since derecognition Taiwan has been actively working to help the USA reduce its trade deficit. In particular Taiwan sees America as its source of arms and arms supplies. Following derecognition there was a one year moratorium on arms supplies to Taiwan but with this over Taiwan is looking to increase its USA arms purchasing.

Within Asia, Japan remains Taiwan's main trade partner although there is concern about the size of Taiwan's trade deficit which has not been helped by the relative depreciation in the value of the Yen. Taiwan enjoys good relations with its ASEAN neighbours although trade is still at a relatively low level and there is competition in searching for world markets for manufactured goods.

An interesting feature of Taiwan's trade is the growth in trade with the People's Republic of China. A small amount of trade has been going for some time in traditional products - such as herbal medicines - from the mainland. With talk of reunification trade has become more open with Taiwan goods being exempted mainland import duties because they were considered 'domestic'. Most of the trade passes through Hong Kong which imports from both the People's Republic of China and Taiwan. Thereafter some estimation is necessary but in 1979 the Hong Kong Trade Development Council estimated that the mainland sold about US$56 million of goods to Taiwan and imported about US$21 million. Taiwan remains openly cautious about growth in trade with the mainland.

For the future, Taiwan's Ten-Year Economic Development Plan sees a major role for foreign trade expansion in the country's economic growth and expects exports of goods and services to grow at an average of 12.4% per annum (in real terms) through the Eighties. It is foreseen that agricultural and processed agricultural products will decline further in their share of exports to 6.7% by 1989 while the industrial products share will rise to 93.3%.

Imports of goods and services are expected to rise at 12.5% per annum in real terms so that by 1989 Taiwan's trade should be balanced with exports of goods and services at US$101.4 billion (at current prices) and imports of goods and services at US$101.2 billion.

The China External Trade Development Council in its booklet 'A Rewarding Venture - 1981' sees Taiwan's elevation of living standards and drive towards higher technology industrialisation as providing a wide variety of market opportunities for overseas companies. Among the specific opportunities specified are:- production equipment and sophisticated components in connection with heavy machinery, petrochemicals, metal working, high technology electronics and telecommunications apparatus, automobile manufacturing, high precision instruments, machine tools, energy conservation, agricultural and industrial raw materials, foreign-made food products and high end consumer products.

11 Labour force

LABOUR FORCE PROFILE

Taiwan has a large labour force with a hardworking image. At the end of 1980 the total population aged 15 years or over stood at 11.4 million of whom 6.7 million were in the labour force. Through the Seventies the labour force has grown at an average annual rate of 3.4%. There is now a shortage of unskilled labour due to a combination of an increase in demand for such labour and a decline in supply (see below). At the end of 1980 unemployment stood at 1.2% having fallen steadily from 1.7% in 1970. About 200,000 workers each year reach the age of maturity and enter the labour force.

Table 111 – **Size of labour force by year**

	1979	1980	('000s)
Total population 15+	**11,084**	**11,378**	
Total labour force	6,507	6,629	
- Employed	6,424	6,547	
- Unemployed	83	82	
Not in the labour force	4,577	4,749	

Source:- Taiwan Provincial Labour Force Survey

Besides its hardworking image, the Taiwan labour force is certainly a well-educated one. In 1968 the government implemented a nine-year public education system which provides free six years of elementary schooling and three years of secondary schooling. Over 95% of workers in 1980 had been educated to this level and the government emphasises the strength of this educational base for further worker training.

The government itself is actively developing labour skills. A 1973 Ministry of Education plan, whose first stage was implemented in 1978, has emphasised vocational education. Its aim was to achieve a ratio of 40:60 between students of senior high schools and those of vocational schools. In addition industrial establishments and trades unions undertake their own educational programmes for workers with vocational skills emphasis.

Table 112 – **High school and vocational school enrolment**

	Second Year	
	1970/71	1979/80
	%	%
Senior high schools	43.2	31.1
Vocational schools	56.8	68.9

Source:-   Ministry of Education

Not only has vocational school enrolment increased disproportionately through the Seventies, there has also been a shift in the colleges and universities from the social sciences and humanities to natural sciences and technology. In 1980 about half of Taiwan's students at tertiary level were enrolled in science and technology courses compared with about 45% ten years earlier.

In addition to vocational schools and higher level education in 1980 the government was operating 654 vocational training centres turning out over 300,000 skilled workers a year.

Table 113 – **Number of students at education levels**

	1980 ('000s)
Total studying in Taiwan	4,577
– Higher education	343
– Secondary education	1,598
– Primary education	2,223
– Pre-school	176
– Other	238
Studying overseas	6

Source:-   Ministry of Education

The rising levels of worker education and a growing demand in the Seventies for unskilled labour has created a short term problem. In the longer run the education level of the labour force is seen as an important ingredient for Taiwan's move to higher technology industries.

Taiwan still has a large pool of adult women from which to draw labour and the ratio of female workers is growing larger. In 1969 there were about four male workers to every female while in 1979 the ratio was three to one.

LABOUR EARNINGS AND CONDITIONS

While the level of labour earnings is still well below that of the main industrialised countries, it has nevertheless been rising quickly and Taiwan can no longer look to a large pool of low cost labour as a base for industrial growth. In 1980 the average manufacturing wage was US$254 per month - an increase of 21% over 1979. The average number of hours worked per month in the manufacturing sector for 1980 was 221.

Table 114 –   Average monthly earnings of employees by industry

Period		Mining & Quarrying	Manufact- uring	Electricity Gas & Water	Construc- tion	Commerce	Transport, Storage & Communi- cations	Others
1973	Ave	2,990	2,525	3,822	2,558	-	3,167	-
1974	Ave	4,618	3,389	5,537	3,669	-	4,413	7,341
1975	Ave	5,252	4,029	6,635	4,302	3,737	5,244	7,848
1976	Ave	6,302	4,707	7,238	4,911	4,036	5,707	8,656
1977	Ave.	6,764	5,544	8,313	5,672	5,441	6,383	9,568
1978	Ave	7,872	6,391	9,422	6,198	6,336	7,257	10,064
1979	Ave	9,243	7,578	11,757	6,919	8,061	8,371	11,790
1980	Ave	11,868	9,154	13,502	8,209	10,411	9,825	11,514

Source:-   DGBAS

In addition to wages many workers would expect to receive fringe benefits in terms of meals, medical care and housing. Most government employees, for example, receive medical care and housing benefits.

The normal week is a 6 day - 48 hour one. Overtime is paid at one and one third to one and two-thirds of the regular wage. After working continuously for one year a worker may take annual leave with pay. The minimum is one week and the maximum one month depending on length of service. If leave is not taken, then double wages and allowances are paid for the holiday period.

The government sets minimum wage levels and a maximum number of hours per day. All workers/employees are entitled to a bonus of one month's wages at Chinese New year.

All workers are compulsorily covered by labour insurance against compensation for maternity, injury, sickness, disability, unemployment, old age and death. 80% of the premium is paid by the employer.

INDUSTRIAL RELATIONS

As one government publication puts it: 'There are no strikes in Taiwan'. The law forbids strikes or destructive acts and any disputes must be submitted to the government for arbitration. As a result there have been no strikes in the last three decades.

The government has set up factory councils - composed of equal numbers of employers and worker representatives - to promote work efficiency and settle labour disputes. This system has been effective in reducing the number of labour disputes. In 1979, 506 disputes were handled successfully by factory councils.

Worker co-operation is also being encouraged by a new and growing system in which workers are allowed to share dividends and buy company shares.

At the end of 1979 Taiwan had 1,593 labour unions of which only six were at national level. Total union membership stood at 999,893 or 15% of the labour force.

LABOUR DEVELOPMENT

Taiwan's Ten-Year Economic Development Plan sees an average yearly increase in the labour force of 2.7% to 1984 and thereafter of 2.3% to 1989. By the end of the Eighties the labour force should have reached 8.31 million. Demand for manpower s planned to grow at the rate at which it becomes available leaving unemployment at around 1.3% for the decade.

Table 115 -   Manpower supply and demand

Item	1979	1984	1989	1980-1984 Av. Annual Increase (%)	1985-1989 Av. Annual Increase (%)	1980-1989 Av. Annual Increase (%)	Av. Annual Increase (%)
Total population (mid-year)	17,339	18,916	20,286	1.8	1.4	295	1.6
Natural increase of population (%)	1.9	1.6	1.2	-	-	-	-
Population aged 15 & over (mid-year)	11,599	13,091	14,398	2.4	1.9	280	2.2
Labour participation rate (%)	58.8	59.2	60.0	-	-	-	-
Labour supply	6,502	7,436	8,312	2.7	2.3	181	2.5
Labour demand	6,418	7,399	8,204	2.7	2.3	179	2.5
Number of unemployed	84	97	108	2.7	2.3	2	2.5
Rate of unemployment (%)	1.3	1.3	1.3	-	-	-	-

Source:-   Council for Economic Planning and Development

In terms of employment structure, increasing job opportunities are seen in the industrial sector and, with more agricultural mechanisation, less agricultural employment needed. By 1984 industrial employment is estimated at 41.8%, with agricultural employment at 17.7%.

Table 116 -   Industrial structure

Sector	1979	1984	1989
		% at current prices	
Gross domestic product	100.0	100.0	100.0
Agriculture	8.9	7.0	5.5
Industry	52.6	55.7	57.7
Mining	1.1	0.9	0.7
Manufacturing	42.8	45.7	47.7
Construction	5.9	6.0	6.0
Electric power and other utilities	2.8	3.1	3.3
Services	38.5	37.3	36.8
Transportation and communications	6.1	6.1	6.1
Other services	32.4	31.2	30.7

Source:-   Council for Economic Planning and Development

Government policies through the Eighties include a continuing reduction in the natural rate of population increase (to below 1.25% by 1989) and a continuing emphasis on vocational training. In general there will be a growing investment in education so that by 1989 education expenditure will account for 5.5% of GNP from 4.1% in 1978.

12 Media and advertising

MEDIA USAGE

In parallel with the growth of the last thirty years in Taiwan's consumer markets there has been a similar dramatic growth in media usage. Literacy has improved with better educational opportunities, television has arrived (in 1962) and newspaper circulation has grown to about 3.3 million per day at the end of the Seventies. Apart from more than 30 daily newspapers there is an abundance of periodicals.

Figures are readily available in Taiwan on publication circulations and numbers of TV and radio sets. However, in this chapter, attention is focussed on the 1981 SRH Taiwan Survey (described in earlier chapters) which provides reliable information on the usage of media by individual people. From an advertising point of view, information based on the individual person's media habits is more useful in identifying promotional opportunities.

Television started in February 1962 in Taiwan with the Education Television Station, and in October of the same year a second network - Taiwan Television Enterprise (TTV) - started broadcasting. In 1969 the China Television Company (CTV) began operations and in 1971 the China Television Service (CTS) started as a development of the original Education Television Station, TTV, CTV and CTS are all private television companies drawing their income from advertising revenue.

Television in Taiwan has developed considerably in a relatively short time. Colour broadcasting began in 1969 and makes up very nearly all of today's broadcasting. The last decade has seen a strong increase in the proportion of Taiwan television that is home produced and Taiwanese television programmes are now useful export earners to countries with sizeable Chinese populations.

Table 117 -   **Profile of Taiwan's television networks**

(End 1979)	TTV	CTV	CTS
Telecast hours			
- Monday to Friday	6 hrs 15 mins	6 hrs 15 mins	11 hrs 52 mins
- Saturday	12 hrs	12 hrs	15 hrs
- Sunday and holidays	13 hrs 15 mins	13 hrs 15 mins	18 hrs 18 mins
Colour programmes	100.0%	100.0%	100.0%
Domestically produced programmes	91.4%	90.6%	91.2%
Programme profile			
- News	21.0%	20.1%	21.0%
- Public Service	10.3%	11.7%	10.1%
- Cultural and education	20.5%	22.6%	20.8%
- Entertainment	45.5%	39.9%	42.1%
- Advertising	6.2%	6.8%	6.0%
Studios	5	5	7
Cameras	21 col	22 col 8 B/W	13 col 6 B/W
Relay stations	10	6	8

Source:-   China Yearbook

Nine out of every ten adults watch television on an average day but the average viewing time is fairly low by Asia Pacific standards at 2.0 hours. The heavier viewers tend to be the young and the elderly. Viewing levels are similar for the three networks in terms of daily viewing with relatively little demographic variation although CTV is stronger with unskilled workers and students. Viewing in rural areas is at about the same level as in urban areas.

Table 118 -   **Summary of TV usage by sex and age**

	Total Adults	Male	Female	15-19	20-24	25-29	30-34	35-44	45+
('000s)	10,497	5,477	5,020	1,377	1,668	1,510	1,193	1,963	2,787
	%	%	%	%	%	%	%	%	%
Watched TV yesterday	91	89	93	93	88	91	88	92	92
Station watched									
- China television	63	62	65	73	63	63	55	61	65
- Taiwan television	63	61	65	65	64	61	54	61	68
- China Television Service	59	58	59	67	55	60	51	56	60

Source:-   SRH Taiwan Survey - 1981

Radio broadcasts began in Taiwan in 1922 and by the end of the Seventies there were 30 radio broadcasting companies with 146 stations and 302 transmitters. Of the 30 companies four were run by the military, 21 by private interests and 5 by public enterprises.

The Government estimate for the end of 1979 is of some eight million radio sets in Taiwan - including tape recorders with a receiver. The SRH Taiwan Survey quoted earlier estimated less than 60 per cent of homes with a set. The implication is of multiple set ownership in homes that have a radio at all.

The lower incidence of radio sets in the home in Taiwan by comparison with Hong Kong and Singapore (over 90% and over 80% respectively) is not reflected in radio listening figures. For example, Taiwan's average daily listening figure of 45% compares with precisely the same estimate of 45% for Hong Kong's adults, and the Singapore figure is similar. On the other hand Taiwan has many more radio stations with over 90 offering a 24 hour service. Taiwan's radio stations broadcast an average of 20 hours a day.

There is not much regional variation in radio listening but it is predominantly an activity of the young/single people and the middle/upper income groups. A higher proportion of men than women listen to the radio: (similar to Hong Kong but the reverse of Singapore).

Prior to the arrival of television, radio in Taiwan largely featured drama series and entertainment. Since the Sixties and TV, radio programming has tended to emphasise music and songs as well as information services such as news reports, traffic information, agriculture and forestry reports.

In terms of audience size the China Broadcasting Station and the Police Broadcasting Station are the clear leaders (both with more than a quarter of adults listening on an average day) followed by International Communication Radio Taipei.

There is one radio broadcasting network offering all English language broadcasts.

Table 119 -   Summary of radio usage by sex and age

	Total Adults	Male	Female	15-19	20-24	25-29	30-34	35-44	45+
('000s)	10,497	5,477	5,020	1,377	1,668	1,510	1,193	1,963	2,787
	%	%	%	%	%	%	%	%	%
Listened to radio									
- yesterday	45	49	40	56	67	56	40	33	31
- in past 7 days	50	55	45	64	73	64	44	37	34

Source:-   SRH Taiwan Survey - 1981

Taiwan has 31 daily **newspapers,** including 2 in English, with a combined daily circulation of 3.3 million in 1979.   In addition there are many newspapers published outside Taiwan sold in the country.

The figures shown below just cover eight leading newspapers so the total average daily readership figure for all newspapers can be expected to be even a little higher. The figures below nevertheless serve to show that newspaper reading is disproportionately male (although relatively more women read a newspaper in Taiwan than in Hong Kong). Readership tends to the lower in the rural areas (59%) and in the South of the country (63%). It is also lower among those aged 45 or over where literacy and education are still something of a problem.

Newspaper readership is dominated by two newspapers - China Times News and United Daily News. Both are estimated to be read by more than a third of the adult population on an average day. The third largest paper - Central Daily News - is read by less than 10 per cent on an average day. The leading paper - China Times - has a wide coverage of finance and economy as well as political and social news. It has a weekly Sunday edition - Sunday Times - and a sister paper - The Commercial Times.

The two daily English language newspapers are the China Post and the China News. Six evening papers are published in Taiwan: Great China Evening News, Min Tsu Evening News, Independence Evening Post, Ching Kung Evening News, Ching Kon Evening News and the English language China News.

The main newspapers of Taiwan and their locations are as follows:

Central Daily News	Taipei
China Daily News	Taipei
Hsin Shing Pao	Taipei
United Daily News	Taipei
China Times	Taipei
Economic Daily News	Taipei
Min Sheng Pao	Taipei
Youth Warrior Daily	Taipei
Mandarin Daily News	Taipei
Commercial Times	Taipei
China News (English)	Taipei
China Post (English)	Taipei
Great China Evening News	Taipei
Independence Evening Post	Taipei
Min Tsu Evening News	Taipei
Chung Cheng Pao	Taipei
Min Sheng Daily News	Taichung
Chung Kuo Daily News	Taichung
Taiwan Daily News	Taichung
Chih Chiang Daily News	Changhua
Shang Kung Daily News	Chiayi
China Daily News (southern edition)	Tainan
Taiwan Times	Kaohsiung
Hsin Wen Pao	Kaohsiung
Chung Kuo Evening News	Kaohsiung
Min Chung Daily News	Kaohsiung
Cheng Kung Evening News	Kaohsiung
Keng Sheng Daily News	Hualien
Chien Kuo Daily News	Penghu
Matsu Daily News	Matsu
Kinmen Daily News	Kinmen

Table 120 –   **Summary of daily newspaper readership by sex and age**

	Total Adults	Male	Female	15-19	20-24	25-29	30-34	35-44	45+
('000s)	10,497	5,477	5,020	1,377	1,668	1,510	1,193	1,963	2,787
	%	%	%	%	%	%	%	%	%
Read daily newspaper* yesterday	75	78	72	79	81	84	79	78	61

Source:-   SRH Taiwan Survey - 1981

* Covers 8 leading newspapers

At the end of 1979 there were 1,772 **magazines** being published in Taiwan (although many of these were house publications). Despite the proliferation of magazines only two have an average issue readership of more than 5 per cent of the population - the weekly Times News and the imported monthly Readers Digest (Chinese language). Both of these publications offer significant cover of white collar workers and urban areas in particular.

Apart from these two there are several womens magazines and television based magazines which offer coverage of a few per cent of adults. From an advertising point of view the remaining small magazines tend to provide specialist media opportunities to specific small target markets. Mass market consumer product advertising very largely goes to television and newspapers.

Table 121 –   **Summary of magazine readership by sex and age**

	Total Adults	Male	Female	15-19	20-24	25-29	30-34	35-44	45+
('000s)	10,497	5,477	5,020	1,377	1,668	1,510	1,193	1,963	2,787
	%	%	%	%	%	%	%	%	%
Weekly magazine* in the past week	18	21	16	26	27	21	18	11	13
Monthly magazine* in the past month	18	17	19	23	29	26	21	11	8

Source:-   SRH Taiwan Survey - 1981

* Covers 9 leading weeklies and 6 leading monthlies

There are a number of imported English language periodicals in Taiwan including several that offer useful cover of businessmen such as Newsweek, Time, Far Eastern Economic Review, Readers Digest.

There is a national organisation - the Magazine Industry Association - which has the aim of promoting the magazine industry in Taiwan.

The **cinema** industry has been encouraged by the Government and has prospered since the late Fifties and Sixties when colour filming started and there was a spurt in film production. Taiwan's Mandarin films, usually based on popular novels or heroic characters, have become popular in Hong Kong and Southeast Asia. In addition Mandarin films shown in Taiwan benefit from a reduced entertainment tax. Approaching 200 Mandarin films are made in Taiwan each year.

In addition to locally made films, leading foreign films are also available in Taiwan cinemas.

Table 122 –   Summary of cinema going by sex and age

	Total Adults	Male	Female	15-19	20-24	25-29	30-34	35-44	45+
('000s)	10,497	5,477	5,020	1,377	1,668	1,510	1,193	1,963	2,787
	%	%	%	%	%	%	%	%	%
Visited cinema									
- in past 7 days	11	14	8	21	25	15	5	3	5
- in past 4 weeks	29	32	25	50	58	45	18	10	11

Source:-   SRH Taiwan Survey - 1981

Despite encouragement given to the cinema industry it has had to contend with rapidly growing competition from colour television. Past week cinema going is at about the same level as in Hong Kong (where 12% of adults were going to the cinema in an average week in 1980) but lower than other countries of the region such as Singapore (26% in the past week) and Philippines (34% in the past month).

In common with cinema goers elsewhere, those visiting the cinema in the past week in Taiwan tend to be male and young adults. The peak age category is

20-24 years. Cinema going is also positively related to educational level reached and negatively related to personal income. It is much stronger in the North of Taiwan (16% in an average week) than in the South or Central areas (8% and 7% in an average week respectively).

The tables below are included to put the leading print media and radio stations into a size perspective.

Table 123 -   **Leading print media**

	Total adults
	('000s) 10,497
	%

Daily newspapers (read yesterday)

1.	China Times News	43
2.	United Daily News	39
3.	Central Daily News	8
4.	Taiwan Hsin Sheng	7
5.	China Daily News	4

Weekly magazines (read in past week)

1.	Times News	13
2.	TV Guide Weekly	4
3.	Show TV Weekly	2
4.	CTS Weekly	2

Monthlies/fortnightlies (read in past month)

1.	Readers Digest	12
2.	Mademoiselle	3
3.	The Crown	3
4.	Sisters Pictorial	3

Source:-   SRH Taiwan Survey - 1981

Table 124 –   **Leading radio stations**

	Total adults
('000s)	10,497
	%

Listened to yesterday

1. China Broadcasting Station	30
2. Police Broadcasting Station	16
3. International Communication Radio Taipei	5
4. Chen Sun Broadcasting Station	2

Source:-   SRH Taiwan Survey - 1981

ADVERTISING EXPENDITURE

Expenditure on advertising in Taiwan is at a fairly low level by comparison with the OECD countries and its more developed Asia Pacific neighbours. For example per capital expenditure in 1978 was four times as large in Singapore and Hong Kong as in Taiwan.

Table 125 –   **Advertising expenditure in the countries of Asia Pacific (1978)**

	Total annual expenditure (US$million)	Expenditure per head of population (US$)
Japan	5,604	49.1
Australia	1,145	81.2
South Korea	277	7.6
Hong Kong	95	20.7
New Zealand	91	28.3
Thailand	86	1.9
Taiwan	**86**	**5.0**
Philippines	77	1.7
Indonesia	57	0.4
Malaysia	55	4.4
Singapore	51	21.9

However, advertising expenditure is growing in Taiwan at a healthy rate. Figures quoted in the China Post show an average growth in advertising expenditure for 1980 of 28% with growth in individual media reported as follows:-

-	Newspapers	36%
-	Magazines	33%
-	Cinema	24%

–	Direct Mail	23%
–	Outdoor	21%
–	Television	18%
–	Radio	15%

13 Retail trade

In 1980 Taiwan's combined retail and wholesale trade accounted for 13.1% of the country's Gross Domestic Product.

With steadily growing consumer spending and - by regional standards - a relatively even distribution of income the retail sector appears poised for solid growth in the short term. Most of the shops are still manifestly short of the merchandising skills which have been acquired by countries with more developed retail sectors. However, space is less of a problem in Taiwan than in some of its Asian neighbours and there are clear signs of improvement in retail practice.

Supermarkets are growing and in 1979 had an annual revenue of almost three billion NT dollars. The Directory of Taiwan (China News) lists 16 supermarkets in Taipei and their names are given below. In 1979 the total number of supermarkets stood at 151 with an average revenue of NT$19.1 million.

Department stores are also commonly found in the urban areas and their total revenue in 1979 was approaching twelve billion NT dollars. In 1979 there were 8,144 department stores with average annual revenue of NT$1.4 million.

A particular feature in Taiwan is the MNDPX stores, which are a kind of co-operative for military and government employees and their families. A wide range of products is carried and at heavily discounted prices. These outlets carry a high volume of retail sales.

Supermarkets in Taipei

Acme Co Ltd -
71 Chunghsiao E Road
Sec 4
Taipei

Chung Hsin Co -
70 Chulin Road
Yungho
Taipei Hsien

Chung Mei Supermarket -
Basement 215 Changan E Road
Sec 2
Taipei

Far Eastern Department Store Ltd -
32 Paoching Road
Taipei
68 Jen Ai Road
Sec 4
Taipei

First Co Ltd -
41 Chunghua Road
Taipei

Galaxy Department Store Co Ltd -
218 Chunghsiao E Road
Sec 4
Taipei

Jen Jen Co Ltd -
90 Chunghua Road
Sec 1
Taipei

Love All Supermarket -
126-1 Chunghsiao E Road
Sec 4
Taipei

Shin Kong Recreation Co Ltd -
12 Nanking W Road
Taipei

Hsin Yi Branch:
230 Hsin Yi Road
Sec 2
Taipei

8 Sanmin Road
Taipei

Shin Shin Co Ltd -
247 Linsen N Road
Taipei

156 Kwangchou St
Taipei

Today's Department Store Co Ltd -
54 Omei St
Taipei

14 Nanking W Road
Taipei

The Industrial and Commercial Census is conducted every five years and this provides basic data on the number and operating conditions of both industrial and commercial establishments. For the intercensal period sample surveys based on the previous census are carried out. The table below is taken from one such intercensal survey (1980) and provides a breakdown of revenue in the wholesale and retail sectors for 1979. Total revenue for the retail sector was estimated at almost 450 billion NT dollars. Net sales in 1979 comprised 96.5% of total revenue.

In April 1981 there were 1.09 million people employed in the commerce sector of Taiwan. The average earnings at the end of 1980 were NT$11,647 per month.

Table 126 –   **Annual revenue of wholesale and retail trade**

1979 Annual revenue (NT$ million)

Total wholesale and retail	**637,063**

Wholesaling:

Agricultural products, livestock, fish	21,972
Food and related products	28,667
Piece goods and apparel	9,441
Construction material	16,736
Furniture and fixtures	3,804
Chemical products	11,043
Paint, polish, dyestuff	2,452
Cleaners and cosmetics	1,738
Medicine and drugs	5,032
Fuels	8,716
Small hardwares	8,501
Machinery	8,984
Electric appliances	11,776
Vehicles and parts	16,748
Instruments	1,649
Watches, eye glasses	5,357
Books, stationery, sports, music	4,419
Goods nec	20,380

Retailing:

Agricultural products, livestock, fish	52,093
Food and related products	49,678
Piece goods and apparel	14,855
Construction material	14,584
Furniture and fixtures	11,176
Chemical products	5,510
Paint, polish, dyestuff	1,870
Cleaners and cosmetics	1,548
Medicine and drugs	13,322
Fuels	11,580
Small hardwares	17,158
Machinery	5,586
Electric appliances	15,877
Vehicles and parts	27,758
Instruments	4,803
Watches, eye glasses	4,394
Books, stationery, sports, music	9,063
Goods nec	12,761
Department stores	11,634
Supermarkets	2,885
Import trading	71,149
Export trading	90,368

Source:-   Ministry of Economic Affairs

Over the period 1971 to 1979 the value of retail sales grew from just over 53 billion Taiwan dollars to just short of 450 billion - a growth rate of 741%. Growth was particularly strong in the latter part of the Seventies.

Table 127 -   **Growth in retail sales**

Annual retail sales (NT$ million)

Year	Annual retail sales (NT$ million)
1971	53,477
1972	81,899
1973	108,074
1974	122,807
1975	151,863
1976	214,925
1977	249,587
1978	415,518
1979	449,647

Source:-   Ministry of Economic Affairs

In 1979 there were 44,780 wholesale establishments in Taiwan and 292,688 retail establishments. In the retail sector the largest category by far is for food and related products outlets of which there are close to ninety thousand. No other single category has more than thirty thousand outlets.

Table 128 -   **Number of retail outlets**

	1979
Agricultural products, livestock, fish	29,267
Food and related products	88,925
Piece goods and apparel	13,716
Construction material	18,189
Furniture and fixtures	7,191
Chemical products	9,209
Paint, polish, dyestuff	1,775
Cleaners and cosmetics	651
Medicine and drugs	17,997
Fuels	6,610
Small hardwares	15,136
Machinery	2,457
Electric appliances	16,382
Vehicles and parts	11,372
Instruments	1,909
Watches, eye glasses	6,471
Books, stationery, sports, music	8,896
Goods nec	20,345
Department stores	8,144
Supermarkets	151
Import trading	1,726
Export trading	6,169

Source:-   Ministry of Economic Affairs

On the catering side, just over 20,000 outlets were estimated at 1979 from the Industrial and Commercial Survey of 1980. Their combined annual revenue was put at 43 billion NT dollars. The figures include more than three thousand hotels and other lodging places.

Table 129 -   **Annual revenue of catering establishments**

	NT$ million Revenue (1979)	Number
Restaurants	11,660	6,492
Eating houses	6,111	6,139
Beverage shops	3,982	3,974
Other drinking and eating houses	10,092	324
Hotels and other lodging places	11,171	3,239

Source:-   Ministry of Economic Affairs

14 Information sources

For a comprehensive listing of over 150 sources of information on Taiwan, the reader is referred to 'Sources of Asian Pacific Economic Information' and 'Sources of Asian Pacific Marketing Information' by Blauvelt and Durlacher (Gower Publishing Company Ltd).

The Taiwan Government and regional bodies provide wide and comprehensive information on all aspects of the economy and life in the Republic. Furthermore, information is usually fairly well up-to-date.

Listed below are some key publications covering both government and private sources.

Principal sources of social, economic and market information

TAIWAN

China Yearbook (annual)	China Publishing Co - Government Information Office
Industry of Free China	Council for Economic Planning and Development
Monthly Statistics of Republic of China	Bureau of Statistics - Directorate General of Budget, Accounting and Statistics
Taiwan Statistical Data Book	Council for Economic Planning and Development
Report on Industrial and Commercial Surveys	Bureau of Statistics - DGBAS
Taiwan - Monthly Industrial Production Statistics	Department of Statistics - Ministry of Economic Affairs
Taiwan - Agricultural Production Statistics (annual)	Department of Agriculture and Forestry
Monthly Bulletin of Labour Statistics	Bureau of Statistics - DGBAS
Yearbook of Labour Statistics	Bureau of Statistics - DGBAS

Monthly Key Economic Indicators of Taiwan	Bureau of Statistics - DGBAS
Monthly Economic Survey	The International Commercial Bank of China
Monthly Statistics of Trade	Inspectorate General of Customs
Monthly Key Social Indicators of Taiwan	Bureau of Statistics - DGBAS
Statistical Yearbook of The Republic of China	Bureau of Statistics - DGBAS
Ten Year Economic Development Plan for Taiwan (1980-1989)	Council for Economic Planning and Development
Economic Progress and Investment Climate in Taiwan	Industrial Development and Investment Centre
Guide to Doing Business with Taiwan	Far East Trade Services
What you Can Sell to Taiwan	" "
What You Can Buy from Taiwan	" "
Energy Outlook for Taiwan	" "
Aviation and Transportation Development in Taiwan	" "
New Incentives and Opportunities for Investment in Taiwan	" "
Legal Considerations and Business Strategy for European Firms Doing Business in Taiwan	" "
Trade Statistics	Minstry of Economic Affairs
A Rewarding Venture - Expanding Sales to the Republic of China	China External Trade Development Council
Economic Development in Taiwan, Republic of China	China External Trade Development Council
Selling in Taiwan	Anglo-Taiwan Trade Committee
Directory of Taiwan	China News (available in hotels)
Guide to Taipei and All Taiwan	Ed. J J Nerbonne (available in hotels)

REGIONAL

Bankers Handbook for Asia	Asian Finance Publications
Asia 1981 - Measures and Magnitudes	Asian Finance Publications
Asia Yearbook	Far Eastern Economic Review

The Taiwan 'Yellow Pages' directory is a useful company reference.

Taiwan addresses

Anglo-Taiwan Trade Committee
36 Nanking E Road
Sec 2 Taipei

Tel: 5214116

Board of Foreign Trade
1 Hukou St
Taipei

Tel: 3510271

China External Trade Development
Council
10th Floor, 201 Tunhua N Rd
Taipei

Tel: 7522311

Council for Agricultural Planning
and Development
37 Nanhai Road
Taipei

Tel: 3317541

Council for Economic Planning
and Development
118 Hwaining St
Taipei

Tel: 3610241

Directorate General of Budget
Accounting and Statistics
1 Chunghsiao E Rd
Sec 1 Taipei

Tel: 3514074

Government Information Office
3 Chunghsiao E Road
Sec 1 Taipei

Tel: 3419211

Importers and Exporters Assoc of Taipei
3rd Floor 65 Nanking E Rd
Sec 3 Taipei

Tel: 5813521

Industrial Development Bureau
109 Hankou St
Sec 1 Taipei

Tel: 3317531

Industrial Development and Investment
Centre
66 Sunchiang Rd
Taipei

Tel: 5717121

Inspectorate General of Customs
85 Hsinsheng S Rd
Taipei

Tel: 7413181

Investment Commission
7th Floor, 73 Kuling St
Taipei

Tel: 3513151

Ministry of Economic Affairs
15 Foochou St
Taipei

Tel: 3517271

Ministry of Finance
2 Ai Kuo W Rd
Taipei

Tel: 3511611

Ministry of Interior
107 Roosevelt Rd
Sec 4 Taipei

Tel: 3415241

Taipei Advertising Association
110-3 Hsinsheng S Rd
Sec 1 Taipei

Tel: 3214817

15 Market research

Being an island of rugged terrain with a number of fairly inaccessible parts it is unusual for research to cover the whole country. It is quite common for research to be restricted to one or more of the main conurbations - namely Taipei, Kaohsiung, Taichung, Tainan and Keelung - which together account for about 28% of the population. However, by regional standards, the rural areas of Taiwan are relatively affluent and there is a strong case for including some rural parts in survey work. The essential constraint is cost.

The authorities maintain excellent records of districts, cities, townships and villages which facilitates sampling across the country. For administative purposes, Taiwan is divided into 5 cities and 16 rural 'hsiens' (counties) including the outlying island, Penghu. The smallest administrative unit for both cities and hsiens is the 'lin'.

As with other Asian countries the standards of market research practice are rather variable. However, it is possible to obtain research of a very high standard, incorporating strictly performed probability sampling, careful questionnaire design and efficient analysis.

Both quantitative and qualitative facilities are available for most common techniques. Syndicated research is now becoming available although at present there is relatively little trend information. Industrial market research is not common although the facilities are available and it is expected to be an area of growing interest for Taiwan through the Eighties.

Fieldwork can be commissioned by itself. Interviewing costs are lower than in Hong Kong and surveys restricted to urban areas are not expensive by regional standards (see below).

About 6 out of 10 homes have a telephone (7 out of 10 in urban areas) but this method of interviewing is not frequently used for surveys of the population at large. Personal interviewing is by far the most common research medium.

Nearly all personal interviewing is in Mandarin or Fukinese (which have the same written form). It is important to take care in translating questionnaires and it is recommended to obtain a back translation from the Chinese before committing to interviewing.

For interviewing at senior levels a high calibre/senior person is normally required: this has implications for cost in financial and industrial research work.

There is no publically available retail audit in Taiwan although research is carried out among retailers who are generally co-operative.

Typical market research costs at the beginning of 1982 are:-

a) Probability sample of 1,000 housewives covering
   the five main cities - 30 minute questionnaire
   - 150 tables and diagnostic report.   NT$600,000

b) 4 group discussions with sample comprising
   20% of total adult population including
   a diagnostic report.   NT$165,000

c) 200 product test personal interviews - one call
   - 50 tables and diagnostic report.   NT$160,000

MARKET RESEARCH COMPANIES

Survey Research Asia Pacific (Taiwan)
66, Fu Hsin North Road
3rd Floor, Tienhsiang Bldg
Taipei (GPO Box 11955)

Tel: 781-6078

Admare
3rd Floor, 56 Sec 2
Chung Shan N Rd
Taipei

Tel: 5632535

PRO
S-1, 4th Floor
Lane 69
Sung Chiang Rd
Taipei

Tel: 5971192

Survey Research Hong Kong Ltd
12th Floor, Block E
Hoi Bun Building
6 Wing Yip Street
Kowloon
Hong Kong

Tel: 3-434181

AVAILABLE RESEARCH REPORTS

SRH TAIWAN SURVEY

The SRH Taiwan Survey quoted throughout this book is available in a number of reports from Survey Research Asia Pacific (Taiwan) Ltd in Taipei or Survey Research Hong Kong Ltd in Hong Kong. Details and prices can be obtained from any Survey Research Group office or from The Asia Pacific Centre.   The following is a list of available reports:- an asterisk indicates that brand data is available.

Demographics; media analysis including TV, newspapers, magazines, cinema, radio; fresh milk*; other liquid milk*, powder milk*; instant coffee*; health food drinks*; grapejuice; blackcurrant drinks; carbonated soft drinks*; juices*; cod liver oil/pills*; hairdressing*; Bovril; chocolate; other confectionery; biscuits; analgesics; vitamin pills*; instant noodles; beer; brandy; Chinese wine; gin; whisky; cigarettes; toiletries; cosmetics; air travel outside Taiwan; infant milk; aerosol insecticide; liquid detergent; toothpaste*; shampoo*; hair conditioner*; disinfectant; toilet soap; powder detergent; radio; colour TV*; black and white TV*; refrigerator*; washing machine*; air conditioner*; car*; motor cycle; telephone; camera*; stereo Hi-Fi; electric sewing machine; video recorder; piano; microwave oven; colour films*; sports played.

TV AUDIENCE RESEARCH

Detailed TV programme ratings are obtained through a panel of homes with a TV meter installed. Reports are available from Admare.

BUSINESS INTERNATIONAL REPORTS

This company offers a range of multi-country business and economic reports, a number of which include Taiwan. These cover such topics as manufacturing costs, executive compensation, business opportunities, economic forecasts, labour surveys, business strategies, money markets, distribution procedures.

ASIAN PROFILES

A major media and marketing survey of upper class men covering eight capital cities including Taipei. The survey was carried out by SRG companies on behalf of Time, Newsweek International and Readers' Digest Association Far East Ltd, from any of whom information can be obtained.

Notes for the tables

- A 'household' is defined as a group of people who sleep under the same roof and normally eat together.

- An 'adult' is a person aged 15 years or over.

- Unless otherwise stated 'income' refers to monthly income. When used as table headings, income categories exclude 'not stated'.

- Population estimates are those applicable at the time of the survey. For the SRH Taiwan Survey the sample population excludes 14% of the total population.

- Percentages have been rounded and may not always add to 100% precisely.

- An asterisk in the body of a table means less than one half per cent. A blank space or dash means zero.

- An asterisk beside a year means the figures are preliminary for the year.

- The letters:-

  NA denote not available for this publication

m.t.	"	metric tonnes
m^3	"	cubic metres
m^2	"	square metres
m	"	metre
DWT	"	dead weight tonnes
Kl	"	kilo litres
hl	"	hectolitres
dz	"	dozen
nec	"	not elsewhere classified

Index